George Lewis Prentiss

A Discourse in Memory of Thomas Harvey Skinner

George Lewis Prentiss

A Discourse in Memory of Thomas Harvey Skinner

ISBN/EAN: 9783743419025

Manufactured in Europe, USA, Canada, Australia, Japa

Cover: Foto ©Lupo / pixelio.de

Manufactured and distributed by brebook publishing software (www.brebook.com)

George Lewis Prentiss

A Discourse in Memory of Thomas Harvey Skinner

A DISCOURSE

IN

𝔐𝔢𝔪𝔬𝔯𝔶 of

THOMAS HARVEY SKINNER, D.D., LL.D.

BY

GEORGE L. PRENTISS,
PASTOR OF THE CHURCH OF THE COVENANT.

ὅτι ἦν ἀνὴρ ἀγαθὸς καὶ πλήρης Πνεύματος ἁγίου καὶ πίστεως.
—Acts, XI. 24.

ANSON D. F. RANDOLPH & CO.
770 BROADWAY, COR. 9th STREET.
NEW YORK:

This Discourse was delivered in the Madison Square Presbyterian Church, New York, on Sabbath Evening, May 7, 1871, and is now published, by request of the Board of Directors and Faculty of the Union Theological Seminary. It was also repeated at Chicago, on the evening of May 25th, before the General Assembly of the Presbyterian Church, by the unanimous request of that venerable body. An Appendix has been added, in which will be found some account of the Funeral, the Addresses made on that occasion, and other matter illustrative of the life and character of Dr. Skinner.

G. L. P.

THOMAS HARVEY SKINNER.

I ESTEEM it a rare privilege to speak to you to-night in memory of the eminent servant of God, who, on the first day of February last, beloved and venerated by us all, departed to be with Christ. His life covered the wide space of almost fourscore years, nearly sixty of which were spent in the public service of his Master. Whether considered by itself as an example of the beauty of Christian holiness, or in its relations with one of the most remarkable periods in the history of the American Church, it is full of interest and instruction. I shall lose no time, therefore, in the way of introduction, but proceed at once to the weighty and grateful task assigned me.

HIS BIRTH AND BOYHOOD.

THOMAS HARVEY SKINNER, son of JOSHUA and MARTHA ANN SKINNER, was born at Harvey's Neck, Perquimons Co., N. C., March 7, 1791. He was the seventh of thirteen children. The plain dwelling, in which he first saw the light, was long since removed by the ever-encroaching waves of Albemarle Sound. The Neck had been the seat of Governor Harvey, whose descendants were now its chief occupants; its society was gay and cultivated, and it had natural attractions fitted to make a lasting impression upon the mind of a sensitive boy. The neighboring woods still abounded with deer and other game, and immense flocks of swans and wild geese swam on the waters both of the sound and of the beautiful Perquimons river, feeding on a sweet grass which then grew on the bottom. When an old man, Dr. Skinner still paid an annual visit to this home of his childhood, and fondly cherished its pleasant memories. The domestic influences in the midst of which he was trained were of the best sort. His parents he described as simple and plain in their mode of life, distinguished for their probity, hospitality and kindness to the poor, beloved and honored by the community, pious and strict in the training and education of their children. His father was by birth a Quaker; his mother was an Episcopalian. After their marriage they became members of the Baptist Church, under the faithful ministry of the Rev. M. Ross. They were both bright examples of spiritual religion, and died in faith and in peace. Their house was much frequented by religious persons, and especially by preachers. It had been furnished as a church, and three Sabbaths out of four the father himself conducted public worship in it; the fourth Sabbath he and his family attended a monthly service in the church, twelve miles distant. He did not preach; he prayed with the people, read the Scriptures to them, and read also a sermon, generally one of the village sermons or one of President Davies'; he united exhortation with the reading; his children conducted the music. It is not strange that God blessed his family greatly, and made him a blessing to his neighbors. Of his thirteen children, twelve reached full age, married and were prosperous. Two of them, a brother and a sister, still survive at a very advanced age.

AT SCHOOL.

Mr. Skinner employed a school-master, of the name of Bailey, in his own house, the neighbors being allowed to send their children also. Under this tutor Thomas was placed at a very early age. Master Bailey was proud of him as a pupil, and boasted of him after he had left the school as a great proficient under his teaching. After having attended awhile two other schools, he was sent to Edenton Academy, then under the care of Mr. Metcalf, an excellent teacher, to whom he at once became affectionately attached, and whose death soon after greatly afflicted and perplexed him. "When I saw his grave, I still had the thought that he must come out of it and be again with us at the academy." Upon the death of Master Metcalf, he passed under the care of Dr. Freeman, who taught him Latin and Greek. He made such rapid progress in his studies, that his eldest brother, Joseph, who was practicing law at Edenton, resolved to take his future training under his own direction; Dr. Freeman was to qualify him for Princeton, and Princeton was to qualify him to be a student of law. This was late in 1804, when he was thirteen years old. He had been living in the family of his uncle John, but was now adopted into that of his brother, under whose roof he remained three years. "I became"—so he wrote more than sixty years later—"as his son. Though himself a young man, he had no equal at the bar; and for intelligence, and talents, and general influence, scarcely any one in the community was his equal. He had married in a family of the highest position a lady of culture and refinement. Her mother, Mrs. Lowther, was a descendant of Governor Eden, the loveliest, most beautiful, most interesting of women. In this family I was a favorite. I remained in it, loved and loving, till I completed my course at the Academy. Greater advantages for the culture of mind and manners I could hardly have desired."

AT COLLEGE.

Let us follow him now to Princeton. He entered Nassau Hall in September, 1807, joining the junior class. This he regarded in later years as a serious mistake. He had been taught Greek very superficially, and had to make up a deficiency in this language. He should, he said, have joined the sophomore class. In his second term, under the tuition of Dr. Maclean, he began to be conscious of having a gift for mathematics—a consciousness he found "unspeakably agreeable," and which seems to have aroused his whole intellectual being to a new life. He conducted himself as a student in the most exemplary manner, being almost never absent from prayers, recitation, or any college exercise, during his entire course. He was supremely desirous of reciting well, and ambitious of a high position in the class, as also of the approbation and favor of the faculty. At the graduation he shared with several others the second honor—a high distinction in one so young, and so imperfectly qualified at the beginning.

A STUDENT OF LAW AT EDENTON.

On his return to Edenton he was welcomed with open arms by the happy family, which had parted with him two years before. "My dear brother's pleasure was at its utmost height and unbounded; I never saw a more delighted person. His love to me seemed to the last degree inventive of means of expression. Had I been his only son, his complacency in me could not have been more demonstrative. Never can I forget his noble, generous, irrepressible sympathy. It was not from the impulse of the moment; it was no less solid and lasting, and full of expedients for my highest worldly advancement, than lively and exuberant. After a thrice happy visit to my parents, and brothers, and sisters at Harvey's Point, I returned to Edenton to commence a law-student, under his training." He continued in his brother's office until the spring of

1811—a space of about eighteen months. This was an exceedingly interesting period of his life. His own reminiscences of it were full of delight. The stimulus to intellectual activity was intense. He not only pursued with diligence his legal studies, and performed faithfully the duties of Clerk of the Superior Court—a place early obtained for him by his brother—but he was ambitious to excel in other directions; he even wrote and published verses. The social influences that surrounded him were fascinating and potent in the highest degree. Some of the most charming and cultivated families of the old North State had their homes in Edenton. The pleasures of its social life, indeed, according to his own account, were very excessive and hindered him not a little in his professional studies.

HIS CONVERSION.

But the hour now approached when social pleasures and the honors of his chosen profession were alike to lose their power over him. God was about to call him to a higher life. His parents, as we have seen, were devoted Christians; and at times the pious atmosphere and customs of the family seem to have excited in him serious thoughts; but it was only for the moment. He describes himself as growing in alienation from God as he grew in years. Neither at the Academy nor at Princeton did he remember to have been under any religious impressions. The whole spirit of college society and sentiment was intensely sensuous and worldly; while few of the students were avowed sceptics, almost every one was a practical atheist. " I left college full to overflow of animal, intellectual, social life, but alienated wholly and fearfully from the life of God, through heart ignorance and blindness.' And in this state he continued until the spring of 1811, when he was on the eve of admission to the bar. It would be wrong to depict the change which now came over him, and over his whole plan of life, in any other than his own exact words:

"A missionary had come to Edenton; he lodged with a friend whom I called to see on Saturday. The missionary, (the Rev. B. H. Rice,) was with us in the parlor. Repulsed by his conversation, and wished him anywhere else than there. The next day he was to preach in the Episcopal church. I heard him with interest greater than I had ever felt in church. In the evening heard him again at the Methodist church, ('*What shall it profit a man, etc.*') Almost overwhelmed with emotion; said to myself, 'Almost thou persuadest me to be a Christian.' I could not sleep till I had done, what I know not that I had done before; knelt in solemn prayer to God. In the morning, before I was out of bed, the servant who attended to my room, announced to me the tidings which had just reached the town, that my brother John had perished by shipwreck! Next to my eldest brother, there was not one of my father's sons more loved and delighted in as a youth of rare promise than he; in mind he was scarcely my eldest brother's inferior. Inexpressibly strong and affectionate was my attachment to him. My brother, my incomparable brother John drowned! Terrible, astounding fact! It shook me to the very centre of my life; coming so close upon nightly impressions received from preaching, it enforced those impressions. Religion became at once my only concern. My brother (J. B. S.) was from home attending court. A week or more elapsed before he returned. It was to me a week of absorption in religious anxiety; night and day, I was praying, reading the Bible, etc.; with constant increase of religious concern. I could attend earnestly to nothing but the salvation of my soul. . . . Near the end of the week there was a transition in my feeling, which I took as hopeful; Scripture had a new face, one passage (Is. 43 : 2.) was inexpressibly consoling to me, the face of the world was new to me; a mild glory was diffused over all nature. I had no distinctness of spiritual perception; no vivid apprehension of Christ as a Saviour; no persuasion that I was converted; but in a vague sense, at least, old things had passed away, and all things had become new. Was full of peace without clear views of evangelical truth, until a minister of the Gospel (the Rev. Mr. Woodbery) who had heard something of what had happened to me, called to see me, and after some conversation with me, told me that he thought I was a Christian. I became unhappy; the question of my conversion had not been in my thought; I now began to consider it, and was filled with misgiving; I could not think the signs of true conversion were with me; I did not know what were such signs; I was full of anxiety about myself, anxiety which did not soon leave me. I attended all the religious meetings; I thought of nothing but religion; I had pleasure in them. A hymn was sweetly sung at one of them,

("Hark, my soul, it is the Lord,") which I heard with singular interest. I was open and fearless in professing myself exercised with religious concern; did not ask what my friends would think of me; was aggressive toward them rather than defensive of myself. But generally I was not at rest in myself; could not assure myself that I had become a Christian."

He then describes his interview with his brother:

"It was a trial severe beyond example in my life. Wished to anticipate reports from others, by informing him myself of the change which had passed over me. He was afflicted by brother John's death, as deeply, perhaps, as myself, but in no degree religiously. He heard my recital with astonishment; I wonder even at this day that I was able to give it to him. . . . . I said to him, 'Don't suppose that, as a matter of course, I am to abandon the study of the Law; I see no inconsistency between the practice of the Law and a religious life.' He made no answer; but seemed profoundly sad, prospecting, doubtless, the end which came. He would talk with me no longer. There was henceforth much diversity in his manner toward me. Sometimes he was severe; I was to be 'a Methodist circuit-rider, going about the country with horse and saddle-bags.' Sometimes he was the ideal of kindness and gentleness: 'Divinity and Law were allies; study Divinity if you will; Hooker's Ecclesiastical Polity was a noble Law-book; go abroad if you will, and perfect yourself in a Divinity School, then return and complete your Law course; you will be all the better accomplished for the bar.' Dearest brother, what was it in me that made my actual course a possibility? All men collectively were as nothing to me compared with this man. What a mystery to me that I could set myself as I did against compliance with his disinterested views and wishes and proposals, for my advancement in the world! If my determination was from aught else than the sovereignty of the Divine Will, the operation of the Holy Spirit within me, it was but proof of perverseness and the basest ingratitude! Infinitely far from this was it intentionally or consciously. Rather would I have displeased all mankind than this one man.

"Five or six weeks passed before I left him. I was not fully satisfied that I had become a Christian. Religious concern was exclusive of every rival feeling. I assumed that all my intimate acquaintances and associates sympathized with me; or that if they did not, it was to their disadvantage. As well as I can remember I had not a single thought of what I might lose of worldly good; all loss from leading a religious life was gain; all good was comprehended in religion. But the question, notwithstanding, was not settled. Was I a Christian? I began to search into the signs of conversion; I read Whitefield's Sermons; I read Edwards on the Affections; I prayed for light from above; at one time I almost thought myself assured, but my doubts returned, and I think I was never absolutely without them when I put the question closely to myself. I made it an objection to my piety, that I had not been vividly and definitely enlightened as to the way of salvation. A passage in Edwards consoled me with the hope that my views on this subject would gradually become more satisfactory; but though generally happy, and immovable in my purpose, I was not certain as to the genuineness of my change."

He then gives an interesting account of his difficulties on the subject of pedo-baptism:

"I became too much agitated internally to weigh evidence; I could not decide absolutely, pro or con, about it. There was to be a public baptism in Edenton, by Uncle Ross, as we called him. About the time of my conversion there was an awakening in the place; seventeen persons, the fruit of it, were to be immersed. The day arrived, a mild and sweet Sabbath day; I heard the preliminary sermon; and went with the solemn procession to the water; they sang hymns as they went; I felt the sanctity and holy beauty of the service; with unutterable emotion I saw the baptism performed; the scene was heavenly. 'Was not this Baptism indeed; the true primitive Baptism?' Had I felt assured that it was so *exclusively*, how gladly should I have been immersed that day! But I did not feel this assurance. From the place I retired into a wood in the neighborhood, and there under the trees, I prayed for divine illumination. Arose from prayer with profound tranquillity of spirit; neither assured nor unassured, but in a frame of soul to which calm reflection was practicable. My scrupulosity was in abeyance; I reviewed the subject, and was at rest as to my personal baptism. Had I not been baptized I might have become a candidate for immersion; but re-baptism was unnecessary, and therefore inexpedient and improper. Thus ended my scruples."

A STUDENT OF DIVINITY.

The next question was, "Shall I change my calling?" He soon solved it by making up his mind to acquire, by the will of God, a theological education, and become a Presbyterian minister of the Gospel. In pursuance of this design, he came to Philadelphia late in the spring of 1811, with the view of putting himself under the care of the celebrated Dr. Ashbel Green; but Dr. Green, on account of the multitude of his labors, declined the request of the youthful applicant, advising him to go to Andover, or else to Princeton, where President Smith was teaching a theological class. He decided in favor of Princeton, and soon after going there joined the Presbyterian church of the place. Among his friends at Princeton was Mr. Scudder, afterwards the distinguished missionary, with whom he had much sweet Christian fellowship. In the autumn of the same year, he was induced to go to Savannah, Ga., where he passed the winter in studying under the eloquent Dr. Henry Kollock. Wm. A. (afterwards Dr.) McDowell, one of his theological classmates at Princeton, was with him also at Savannah. Dr. Kollock's instruction was not of much advantage to him. In the spring of 1812, he came to Elizabethtown, N. J., having accepted the friendly invitation of Rev. (afterwards Dr.) John McDowell to become a member of his family and his theological pupil. He remained under the roof of this admirable man for seven months; and in after years, even to old age, he recurred to this period of his life with the utmost satisfaction and thankfulness. Probably there was at that time no Presbyterian minister in the whole country, with whom he could have studied to more advantage. Besides being one of the best preachers of his day, Dr. McDowell was a model of pastoral care and faithfulness; his piety was as wise and tender as it was earnest; rare domestic virtues rendered his home a sweet and hallowed place. In the bosom of this lovely Christian family, he was not merely the student of divinity; here he learned also how a good man can bear affliction, and illustrate the cheerful submission, patience, and gentleness of the Gospel.

While pursuing his studies at Elizabethtown, he took an active part in the religious meetings of the place. The Rev. Dr. Hatfield has kindly furnished me with extracts from an old diary kept by an officer of Dr. McDowell's church, which bear witness on this point. Let me read some passages:

Aug. 9, 1812.—" In evening at Adelphian Society. The assembly was so great, although I was in pretty good season, I could get only in the entry. Mr. Skinner read Edwards' sermon on the punishment of the wicked." Aug. 16.—" In evening at Adelphian Academy; a full house. Mr. Skinner read Davies' sermon on lukewarmness in religion." Sept. 6.—" In evening, Mr. Skinner read Mr. Whitefield's sermon, *Lord, Lord, open to us.*" Sept. 13.—" In forenoon, heard Mr. Skinner read Mr. Edwards' sermon from ' Their feet shall slide in due time.' P. M. Heard Mr. Skinner read a sermon from ' Rejoice not that the devils are subject to you,'" etc., etc.

Tuesday evening, Oct. 13.—" At society at R. Price's. Rev. Wm. A. McDowell, Mr. Skinner, and Elihu Price spoke. A solemn meeting." Sab., Oct. 25.—"In evening went with Mr. Skinner to the black society in African street. I spoke after him from the 55th chapter of Isaiah." Sab., Dec. 13.—"In evening, at Society Adelphian Academy. Mr. Skinner read Davies' sermon. Mr. McDowell spoke; afterward Mr. Skinner, from 'What think ye of Christ?' applied to all."

IS LICENSED AND BEGINS TO PREACH.

On the following Wednesday, December 16, 1812, he was licensed to preach the Gospel by the Presbytery at Morristown. He came to Newark with Rev. (afterwards Dr.) Richards on the afternoon of the same day, and in the evening preached his first sermon, in the First Presbyterian Church, from the text, Luke 12: 32. *Fear not, little flock*, etc., etc. The ride from Morristown to Newark on this winter afternoon almost cost him his life. He contracted a cold, which settled upon his lungs, and before the close of another year brought him to the verge of the grave. But nothing, at that time, could dampen the ardor of his spirit.

Friday, Dec. 18 (I quote again the old diary).—"At Academy. Mr. Skinner spoke for the first time on the jailor. A crowded house." Sab., Dec. 20, A. M.—Mr. Skinner, from Matthew 27: 67. 'Who also himself was Jesus' disciple.' He described the character of a Christian: 1. He is born again. 2. Repenteth of his sins. 3. Believeth in Christ. 4. Loveth God supremely. 5. Loveth his neighbor. 6. Has the same mind in him, viz., humble, obedient, etc., etc. 7. Is not conformed to the world; hateth sin." Tuesday, Dec. 22.—At R. Price's. Mr. Condit preached. Mr. Skinner and Mr. McDowell spoke afterwards. Meeting solemn."

He now set out on his return to the South. The last Sabbath in December he passed in Philadelphia, preaching in the Tabernacle, Ranstead's Court, for the Rev. Mr. Joyce. It was an obscure place, but his name had already become known; and after the sermon he was waited upon by representatives of the powerful Second Church, Arch street corner of Third, who urged him to preach for them on the next Sunday, January 2, 1813. He consented to do so, and this was his first introduction to the congregation of which he was soon to become a pastor. After preaching here several weeks, he resumed his journey homeward. The first Sabbath in February he spent in Washington; and an extract from the memoir of Dr. James Milnor, the revered rector of St. George's Church in this city, who was then a member of Congress, will show how he spent it:

"His next letter contains an account of a visit to Washington, on his way from Philadelphia southward, of a young Presbyterian preacher, the Rev. Mr. Skinner, who brought him a letter of introduction from Mr. Bradford, and whose eloquent and faithful preaching at the capital left a deep and most salutary impression. Mr. Milnor thus narrates two incidents connected with this visit: 'Feb. 8, 1813.—An amiable friend of mine'—apparently a fellow-member of Congress—' who would have been much offended to be told he was not a believer, was frank enough to acknowledge to me that he went home after morning service, retired to his chamber, and wept bitterly at the reflection that, at the age of fifty, this young stripling should have so laid open his deformities, and set before him truths to which he had so long been experimentally a stranger. A conversation held with him to-day induces me to believe that an abiding impression has been made upon his mind. On Sunday afternoon, at the close of service, a lady who had been much affected went to speak to Mr. Skinner; but her tears choked her utterance, and she withdrew.'"*

I think you will agree with me that this record not only shows his early zeal and pungency as a preacher, but betokens also the depth and power of his early religious experience. He was still in his twenty-second year, and had been converted less than two years, when his preaching arrested such attention in the gay and thoughtless capital of the nation.

IS ORDAINED PASTOR OF THE SECOND CHURCH IN PHILADELPHIA.

After visiting his friends in North Carolina, he returned to Philadelphia, and on the 10th of June, 1813, was ordained co-pastor with Dr. Janeway of the Second Presbyterian Church, Arch street. In this position he remained three years and four months. It was the most trying period of his ministerial life. The religious

---

* Memoir of Dr. Milnor, pp. 142–3.

atmosphere was charged with suspicion and strife. Differences of opinion about ability, about the use of means and measures, about the question whether men ought to be addressed as saints, sinners and seekers, or only as saints and sinners, about unregenerate praying, lay-exertion, or "lay-preaching," as it was called, and other points, began to agitate the community and to array the Presbyterian ministers and churches on opposite sides. This is not the place to go into the history of these sharp contentions. They raged for several years with a violence which seems to us now scarcely credible. The most eminent clergymen and laymen of the Church took part in them, they were talked about at the corners of the streets, and the meetings of Presbytery and Synod were sometimes wrought up by them to a high pitch of excitement. It was not in the ardent nature of the junior pastor of the Second Church to act the part of a neutral at such a moment. Indeed, a change in his own views seems to have been, in part, the occasion of the conflict. He accordingly threw himself into it with his whole heart. He became one of its leaders and fought the battle with the dashing energy and courage of a youthful hero. Dr. Green, now President of Nassau Hall, Dr. Janeway, and many of the most influential members of his church were against him; Rev. James Patterson, the fervid evangelist, Dr. James P. Wilson, a master in the Presbyterian Israel, and another portion of the Church were for him. But he was not happy; he felt himself in the wrong place; the ruling influences were not friendly to him; and in November, 1816, the Presbytery dissolved his co-pastoral relation with the Second Church. I have alluded to a change in his theological views.

"I became (he says) an Edwardean, though not, as was charged on me, a *Hopkinsian*, in doctrine. Not opposition to Edwards, but vagueness and indistinctness about the nature of virtue and the freedom of the will, had appeared in my preaching. My theological training was defective. I preached confusedly and incoherently on the means of grace. I encouraged and urged unregenerate praying, or waiting for the Spirit. I did not understand, that though the simple movements of nature are to be stimulated, no delay of repentance should be admitted; that holy affections and actions should instantaneously follow thought on their objects; that impenitence after this thought is aggravated rebellion. Through acquaintance and conversation with such men as Dr. Richards, Dr. Griffin, Dr. Payson, and especially with Dr. S. H. Cox, (now a student in Philadelphia, full of intelligence, brightness, and zeal,) I became reflective on myself as a preacher, and saw, as in a sunbeam, the error of my way. My preaching on the doings of unregeneracy was revolutionized; my 'new light' filled it. It was not yet pure or complete in its radiance; had it been, perhaps the consequences which followed, might not have had place; but such as it was, I imparted it without restraint; I could not forbear; to make any allowance to impenitence after the hearing of the gospel, was to be myself disloyal to truth and grace. I protested against it with the utmost of my strength. * * * I wrote a piece on the subject which made my preaching so troublesome; and on its appearance in one of the papers, Dr. Alexander, of Princeton, not knowing its author, pronounced it just. And at the request of Professor Hodge, I amplified it for publication in the *Princeton Repertory*, where it may be seen. But my thoughts on it, at first, were not perfect, though on the way to perfection; I was right in condemning the doings of the unregenerate; I was defective in not discriminating between them, and the exercises of simple nature which are generally in order to those of personal holiness."

Nearly fifty years later he passed his own judgment upon his first pastorate in Philadelphia. It is a gem of Christian humility, candor, and magnanimity. Let me quote a few sentences:

"A retrospect of my ministry in the Second Presbyterian Church from my present standpoint in time convinces me of uncommon imperfection in it, from first to last. I fear I was in 'rash haste' to undertake it. But two years and four months had passed, from the date of my conversion; I was in the early part of my twenty-second year; the church was among the first, if not the first of all, of the Presbyterian order; my predecessor was a patriarch and ruler in it, of high distinction. I had indeed a coadjutor, and this was urged as a reason which might well be decisive. But, nevertheless, my accepting the call was a great venture; and that the result was not my ruin, was of the amazing grace of God. How ought I to praise Him that I escaped from the severe ordeal to serve Him, in the ministry, for nearly half a century afterwards!"

If he had been the only pastor, and had not been interfered with from without, the change in his preaching would not, he thinks, have displaced him; but the unfriendly influences he had to work under, made him too "erect and indignant."

"My preaching was positive, unpliable, authoritative, heedless of its bearing on my position; there was too much of severity and terror in it, too much of rough dealing with the old doctrine about unregenerate prayers, waiting, etc.; too little consideration of my youth and experience; too little unction and gentleness."

HIS PASTORATE IN LOCUST STREET.

Soon after his dismission from the Second Church he accepted a call to the Fifth Presbyterian Church, in Locust street; its pastor, the Rev. J. K. Burch, having just resigned. He was installed December 1, 1816. And now began the second period of his ministry in Philadelphia; a period in extreme contrast with the first. The church in Arch street ranked among the foremost in all the land for intelligence, character, wealth, orthodoxy, and influence; its voice was potential in ecclesiastical affairs. The church in Locust street was hardly known, even in its own city; its membership was small, poor, and without the slightest pretension to culture of any sort; its meeting-house, a wretched, unsightly building, liable to be blown down by the first storm, in an obscure out-of-the-way place, and burdened with a debt exceeding its value.

Into this valley of humiliation the successor of Dr. Green, in the Second Church, went down in company with about seventy of his old flock, who refused to part from him. They expected to stay in Locust street only a short time; but they stayed there in fact more than six years. They fell into the error which has often been committed. They tried to unite uncongenial elements, and build up a vigorous church out of an old, enfeebled organization. It would have been much better had they formed a new church out of the new homogeneous materials. The consequence of this mistake was that the Locust street people, very differently trained, and belonging to another sphere in life, did not coalesce with those who came from Arch street. Numbers of them left and joined themselves to their former pastor, who had meanwhile returned to the city. The disadvantages and trials of the situation were insuperable, and they increased from month to month. For some years almost no salary was paid; people who liked the preaching did not like it well enough to identify themselves with such a sinking, hopeless cause. The whole movement seemed from first to last to be only a dead failure. The crisis at length approached, when it would be necessary to sell the building in order to pay arrears for ground-rent.

About this time the Presbyterian church in New Orleans, whose pulpit had been made vacant by the death of the youthful and eloquent Sylvester Larned, called the pastor of the Locust street church to take his place. He declined the call on condition that another edifice should be built for him in a better locality. This was agreed to. Providence signally favored the undertaking; and on June 8, 1823, the new house of worship on Arch street, near Tenth, was dedicated, Dr. Miller, of Princeton, preaching the sermon.

And now let me give you some of Dr. Skinner's own reflections on this portion of his ministerial life:

"I was far happier and of better courage than I had been; and, on the whole, my mistake, if I made one, turned out to my unspeakable advantage. I had acquired, through the influence of my new theological views, an independence and energy of thinking, and an ability and delight in preaching, to which I was profoundly a stranger before. My preaching had been meagre, commonplace, superficial; it had troubled no one; it was generally acceptable, but it required on my part little vigor of thought, and neither presupposed nor promised improvement; it was becoming irksome; it made no use of the infinite affluence of theology; it had little to do with the mines of the Inspired Word; its material was what lay on the surface, it had been used again and again; and it almost seemed that nothing new was left; that I had nearly exhausted the substantive matter of preaching. New topics there were, but I had little really new to say about them. I fear my ministry would have culminated in commonplace, but for the impulse it received from the theological novelty, which cost me my loss of position. All, however, was henceforth new in my work. I became a thinker; I threw off the incubus of servility to tradition and ecclesiastical authority; I revelled in the consciousness of being myself; I saw myself amidst infinite treasures of divine knowledge and wisdom, which a thousand lives would be too short to begin to appropriate. My mind was aglow with interest; its life and activity could not be suppressed; intense application became its law, its habit, its unspeakable pleasure. Thus changed in the inner man, I began my Locust street labors. My ministry there was the seed-time of that harvest which, by the grace of God, I have been garnering up to the present day. It was well attended by persons who did not join the church—persons of intelligence and influence. It was fruitful in the religious community. It prepared the way for great success in the sequel of my Philadelphia course. Having a small parish, I had time for study and writing. I have made few discourses better than those which I preached in this poor place."

HIS ARCH STREET LABORS.

We come now to the third and longest period of his ministry in Philadelphia. He had fairly won his way to a position of the highest personal and theological influence. The day of his humiliation was past. He was once more in Arch street, the sole pastor of a strong and united church. His people were devotedly attached to him, and the whole Christian community held him in honor. A day of uncommon success and spiritual prosperity had dawned. Soon after entering the new sanctuary, he began a series of Sabbath evening discourses upon the Sermon on the Mount. Large crowds flocked to hear them. The course ran through a whole year, but the house was filled to the last, and the interest rather increased than abated. No sooner was this course finished, than he announced a doctrinal series, with the design of acquainting the people of Philadelphia, as far as he might be able to do so in this way, with the dogmatic differences between himself and those who had charged him with unsoundness in the faith. He took this step, not without misgiving, both in his own mind, and on the part of some of his friends. There would be no more crowded assemblies to hear him, it was said. Sermons on doctrines! Alas! for such imprudence. But he was fixed in his purpose. "Prejudice against doctrinal preaching," was the subject of his first discourse. The house was, if possible, fuller than ever. The next evening it was crowded as before. The third evening it was still filled to overflowing. And so on to the seventh, when the subject was, "Original Sin." This sermon caused some theological commotion, and led even to talk about a trial for heresy; but he was not molested. "From this time and onward to the end of the course, I doubt not the house would have been overfull, if its capacity had been threefold larger. Such eagerness to hear doctrinal preaching! The course was extended through six months. Its effect was very great, both upon the Presbyterian sentiment of the city, and upon the Christian public at large. "The doctrine I had preached was, for substance, reproduced in the ministry of Mr. Patterson, a mighty revivalist, and a mighty man of God. Its reproach had rapidly passed away, and my reproach with it. Testimonies of confidence came to me from almost every quarter. The ministers of Newark, Dr. Richards, Dr. Griffin, Dr. Spring, of New York, eminent ministers in New England, in the West, near and remote, gave me warm expressions of sympathy. I stood well with the Princeton professors. I was made one of the Directors of the seminary, Dr. Green nominating me to the Assembly for the place. I had become popular. . . . . My preaching was blest. It was the means of establishing and extending what there was of peculiarity in my views. It laid the foundation for large success in the eight following years of my ministry in Philadelphia."

His labors during these eight years would afford ample material for an entire volume. Should a full account of them ever be published, it will be regarded, I do not doubt, as one of the most striking chapters in the annals of the American pulpit and pastoral experience. Richard Baxter, in the palmy days of his Kidderminster ministry, could hardly have surpassed him in abundance of preaching, or in intensity of zeal and devotion to the work of saving souls. The period was marked by scenes of spiritual refreshment and power truly pentecostal. His own reminiscences of it a third of a century later, were extremely vivid. How his face shone, and how his eye beamed with the old joy, as he recalled the years 1827, 1830–1–2, and rehearsed the wonderful works and manifestations of the

Spirit of God, which rendered those years forever memorable. It was a time of great revivals of religion all over the land. That of 1831–2 was especially powerful and wide-spread. How many of its converts are still busy in the vineyard of the Lord! Dr. Skinner threw his whole soul into the movement. He held "protracted meetings," as they were termed, in his own church, and even adopted two of the so-called "new measures," although he was not, technically speaking, "a new measure" man. One of the measures was to detain persons exercised under preaching, after service, for further action with them; the other, a meeting for private inquiry on a future occasion. His course, as to the former, comprised generally a pointed address to the persons before him, a prayer in which they were requested to indicate determination, if they had formed it, by standing up; and afterwards, conversation with them individually. At the inquiry meeting, he usually made an address to all present, after which he conversed with them one by one, passing from place to place. He speaks of having seen "wondrous results" from both these expedients, and gives several instances. Here is the first of them: "One evening, after sermon, I invited those who remained to come up to the desk before the pulpit. A young man was in the gallery, to whom a religious friend near him said, after the invitation had been given, 'Now, T——, is your time.' The young man came from a distant seat, walked the whole length of the middle aisle, under the intensely interested notice of every eye; and, behold, when he arrived at the desk, his mother, coming from a neighboring pew, took her stand by his side. The mother and son joined the church. The son has been, for many years, an eminent minister of the Gospel."

REMARKABLE CONVERSIONS.

During the revivals of 1827 and 1830-2, some very striking conversions took place under his preaching. One of them—that of the distinguished pastor of the Broadway Tabernacle, in this city—has just been mentioned. Another was that of the late Wm. T. Dwight, D. D., for many years pastor of the Third Congregational Church, in Portland, Me.—a man worthy of his descent from the two most illustrious Presidents of Yale and Nassau Hall, and, in his day, one of the leading ministers of New England. Mr. Dwight was, at the time, a lawyer in Philadelphia. He had already won distinction at the bar and in the literary world. Dr. Skinner has left on record a deeply interesting account of his conversion.*

"He was my hearer more than eleven years; and the anticipation of his presence in my audience was always to me a special stimulant and a regulative power in my preparations for pulpit work. . . . . . I think my ministry was not spiritually profitable to him until the

* See Prof. Smyth's Sketch of the Life and Ministry of Dr. Dwight, pp. 9-13.

spring of 1831. He was, so far as I know, more tender to the personal bearing of divine truth, when he first came to the city, than he was afterwards, until then. At my interview with him, immediately after his arrival, he desired me, with tears, to be faithful to him in pastoral attentions; but when some years afterwards, at a season of special awakening in the church, I conversed with him intimately on the state of his soul, I thought some of my remarks were scarcely welcome to him. He was reserved and distant, and I soon withdrew. Perhaps my manner was not altogether right, but I was quite discouraged, and did not soon repeat this kind of conference with him, and, probably, should never have done so, had he not taken the initiative at his conversion. There was a powerful revival of religion in the church when this occurred. He had become engaged to be married to a member of our communion, an eminently pious and estimable young lady; she became intensely anxious for him, and not less so for herself, as espoused to a man whom she regarded as unregenerate. She called on me to confer with me about him, and about her duty in respect to him. We had a Wednesday evening gathering, at which there had been very remarkable manifestations of the Holy Spirit's presence. Though I knew he was not interested in night-meetings, and did not like such extemporaneous addresses as I was wont to make at them, I advised her to induce him, if possible, to attend this service, and to keep a fast with reference to his conversion at it. She followed my advice. At the next occasion of it, if I remember well, Mr. Dwight was among the attendants, he sat remotely from the desk, in the shade; and I did not see him until the preliminary devotions were finished;

and I should, perhaps, not have noticed him, but for the green spectacles which he wore to soften to his delicate sight the brilliancy of the chandeliers by which the room was lighted. I was startled with surprise, having forgotten that I had given the advice to my young friend, of which I have spoken, and never having seen him before, I think, at a night-meeting; but now it occurred to me, with great force, as a motive and as implying an obligation to carry out, if possible, by the grace of God, the object of it. It was on arising to speak that I first saw Mr. Dwight. Instantly I determined, agitated as I was with concern, to make my remarks bear directly on the single point of his being, through the power of the Spirit, here and now brought to Christ. I believe God enabled me to form the determination, and assisted me in fulfilling it. My impromptu address was short; but, though I knew not this till the third day afterwards, it was effectual. We had a meeting the ensuing Friday evening, when I was to preach our weekly lecture. I had no thought of seeing Mr. Dwight among my hearers; but on entering the house I was again troubled by seeing him, not as before, sitting at a distance in the shade, but close to the pulpit, directly under the blaze of a chandelier. His appearance indicated, palpably, that he was deeply excited; and I, too, was excited, as I have not often been, with a sense of my responsibility, and with fear that I was not prepared to meet it. I had premeditated a discourse on Acts xiii. 41: 'Behold, ye despisers, and wonder and perish; for I work a work in your days, a work which ye shall in no wise believe, though a man declare it unto you.' My purpose was to alarm, if possible, persons who, at such a season of grace as God had granted to our

Church, were without concern for their salvation. As respected what I assumed was Mr. Dwight's case, I thought this a very unseasonable design; but I was shut up to it; I could treat no other theme. The perturbation of my mind disqualified me from treating this aright, and I was greatly discontented with my lecture. My manner seemed to myself harsh and severe, and to the last degree unsuitable to persons in the state of feeling of which I was sure Mr. Dwight was the subject. In accents of unusual alarm and terror, I thundered the divine indignation against the indifferent; but my principal endeavor in the discourse was to set forth the surpassing glory of the work of God, then going on amongst us; whence, to its practical despisers, the infinite peril denounced in the text; and, as appeared the day following, I was in this part of my labor speaking a word not out of season to him who that night engrossed my anxiety. I dismissed the assembly with the liveliest self-dissatisfaction, thinking I had abused one of the best opportunities of doing good ever afforded me. The next morning, at about eight o'clock, Mr. Dwight called at my house, and told the servant to ask me if I could see him during the day; and, if I could, to say at what hour he should call again. I requested him to come to me at eleven o'clock. He was in my study punctually at that hour; but he sat several minutes in silence, weeping profusely, his face swollen with previous emotion, and his whole frame indicating sorrow such as I have hardly seen in my whole experience in the ministry. At length, with a suffused countenance, and with a low, hesitating voice, he said: "I have scarcely slept since Wednesday night; I was induced to attend the meeting by my friend; till that evening, I had, it seems to me, never heard the Gospel; my feelings have been strange and wonderful; I know not how it is with me, but your sermon last night was a perfect balm to my soul.' I was astonished, but he went on to say that it was the transcendent glory of the work of the Spirit, as depicted in the discourse, that gave him consolation; and I thought that a spiritual apprehension of this, even under my imperfect representation of it, might sufficiently explain his new experience. I could have no doubt that he had been born of the Holy Spirit. Our conversation continued for some time. He at length left me, happier than I can tell, to go on with my preparations for the pulpit on the morrow. Truly, I was 'like them that dream.'"

There were other cases, hardly less striking; but I have no time to dwell upon them.

THE YEAR 1827.

I must, however, refer again to the year 1827, which Dr. Skinner regarded as the most deeply spiritual of his ministry. His own record of some of the scenes which he witnessed during this year, is singularly interesting. The work began in his study:

"Spiritual decline in the parish had become insupportably deep and predominant. In February, or early in March, two brethren, with whom I had conversed on the state of religion, met with me in my study at about six o'clock, A. M., for prayer. We passed an entire hour on our knees, one following another in confession and supplication. We arose under a strange impression: think we were filled with the conflicting and humbling influences of the Spirit: talked together for a few moments, and parted with the expressed purpose and agreement that we would see others of the church, speak to them of the necessity of a change in our spiritual condition, and, if they sympathized with us about this, inquire whether they would like to attend an early meeting for prayer with a few others; and if they were quite in earnest, to invite them to be with us the following morning. Seventeen assembled, every one like-minded with the rest, all of us on our knees one hour, praying one after another as self-prompted to do so, without rising. Agreed together to extend our application to others, after the same manner as at the first meeting, and to meet again the next morning. Not less than sixty were present; every one, so far as we can judge, in the same state of feeling. The concern was to the last degree lively and deep. The place (my study) was too strait. Privacy was no longer practicable; a morning meeting for prayer at six o'clock was announced; the place, a room in the church. The concern became notorious; and its character was in keeping with the spirit of the study meetings. A fast-day was agreed upon. The room in the church was filled at nine o'clock. I have never been at a meeting of equal interest. It was stated at the beginning that there had been no predetermination as to the duration of the meeting. It might be continued longer than usual. If for domestic or other reasons persons needed to withdraw, they could do so, and, if they pleased, return. For a much longer time than common, the services were exclusively singing, prayer and reading the Scriptures. They were strangely interesting; the Spirit, apparently, was in them; they were as powerful preaching. The Word was luminous with its inherent light; the worship, in every part, was wonderful; the susceptibility of the people, the impression of divine things upon them, was wholly unexampled in all my experience, before and since. The truth in bare texts of Scripture, in verses of hymns, in utterances in prayer, was quick, powerful and as a two-edged sword. An assembly so moved I have never seen. There was no noise, no visible agitation, but an emotional stillness like that of grief at its lowest depth. No outward, audible expression could equal the feeling or have any place as revealing it.

"At length I began to preach. The chief of my points was: The means of actualizing a work of the Spirit in the church. When I was speaking, not before, I think, a renewal of our covenant as a church occurred to me as an appropriate means. I resolved to propose it, and sent the sexton to bring the book containing the covenant. After preparing the way carefully, the solemn act was to be performed. Two of the brethren arose, one after the other, and with flowing tears said they could not join with us in it. They had broken this covenant; the guilt of doing it was upon them; they trembled at the proposal which had been made; so they declared in tearful, thrilling accents! How was the meeting moved! A brother, greatly esteemed, and, as I am persuaded, now filled with the Spirit, arose and, in the name of the whole meeting, offered a prayer for the two who had dissented. I have that singular prayer still in remembrance, almost as if I had just now heard it. What a soft, subdued, melting, just audible voice, full of love, like the dew of Hermon! He said to the Lord: Let these brethren understand that they cannot release themselves from their covenant bonds; that, renew them or not, they were irrevocably under them; that their having broken them demanded repentance, but could not justify disowning them. Then he most touchingly implored that they might be induced to change their purpose and unite with us in the holy transaction. I proceeded; the covenant was read; the meeting promptly entered into it anew; the two brethren still declining. I will not attempt to describe the emotion with which we were all filled. My sermon—not shorter than two hours, I am quite sure, longer, I think, rather than shorter — was finished; at four o'clock the meeting was dissolved."

The interest continued almost unabated to the end of the year. The number of conversions was not, indeed, as large as in subsequent revivals; but the spiritual life of the church, as manifested in brotherly love, unity, fellowship, delight in Christian ordinances and co-operation in Christian work, developed itself in marvellous power.

CALL TO BOSTON.

Early in 1828 Dr. Skinner was called to the Pine street church in Boston. The contest with Unitarianism in the old Puritan capital was then at its height. Dr. Beecher, who had come from Litchfield for that very purpose, was waging it with all the energies of his great soul, and he entreated Dr. Skinner to come and assist him in the struggle. The Rev. Dr. Wisner, one of the weightiest men in New England, was sent to Philadelphia to plead the cause of the Pine street church and of orthodoxy in Boston. Dr. Ashbel Green seconded his appeal to the Presbytery; and in spite of the protest and lamentations of the Arch street church, the call was put into the hands of Dr. Skinner and accepted. It is a curious circumstance that he had scarcely been installed in Boston, when Dr. Beecher was called to the vacant pulpit in Philadelphia. "I got Skinner a call to Boston, and he came. His congregation, to be up with me, gave me a call to his place, and got several persons to write urgently. Among others, Dr. Miller, of Princeton, wrote an argument, very strong, and when it was read on my trial at Cincinnati it made a sensation."*

Dr. Skinner remained in Boston a few months only. The climate proved unfriendly. He had accepted the call, in part, for the sake of his health, now seriously impaired; but his health grew worse instead of better; he

---

* Dr. Beecher's Life. Vol. II., p. 133.

Dr. Beecher's account of the visit made to him by a committee of the Arch street church is highly characteristic, and throws light upon the religious and theological temper of the times. "When the two gentlemen came on to see me about the call, I took them into my inquiry meeting. There was great variety of cases. Language of simplicity came along, and they'd see me talking 'way down in language fit for children, and then, the next moment, rise up into clear, strong, philosophical language. And then the language of free agency and ability came along, and then, they told me afterward, they thought I was going to be a—what d'ye call it?—Arminian, and they'd stick up their ears. I *made something* of free agency — more than a Calvinist would do usually—and brought folks up to *do* what they were able to do. But next minute came along the plea of morality and self-dependence, and I took them by the nape of the neck and twisted their neck off. So they saw that I had my replies according to the subject, and in the course of the evening heard me touch on seven or eight or more different states of mind."

sighed after his old friends in Arch street, while they were still mourning over his absence from them; and, accordingly, at their earnest entreaty and under the promise of an assistant, in the autumn of 1828 he returned to Philadelphia and resumed his pastorate among them.

"My 'deportation to Boston,' as Mr. Barnes has called my transference thither, (so he wrote a third of a century later,) was no disadvantage, as far as I know, in any respect. It was, in effect, a blessing to Pine street; and it was an advantage to myself. It was the means of acquainting me better with men; it brought me into more intimate relations with Dr. Beecher, one of the first of American ministers, and an eminent man of God whom it was a privilege to know well; it was an admirable discipline to my spirit; it taught me to estimate more justly my dear Arch street church. It was to them, too, a benefit. It prepared them to receive me, on my return to them, with a lively renewal of interest in me and in my pastorate. I did not delay my return. With a heart overfull of joy and thankfulness, I resumed my ministry among them. There was great joy in the whole church and congregation. What a happy people! what a happy pastor!"

For a while after his return he was assisted by the Rev. Samuel Stearns, an admirable man, whose early death was a severe loss to the American church. During the memorable years 1831–2, he was greatly aided at different times by the Rev. Joel Parker, then in the full glow of his evangelistic zeal and power; and also by the Rev. Edward Beecher, in conjunction with whom he prepared the excellent little work entitled, "Hints designed to aid Christians in their Efforts to convert Men to God."

AT ANDOVER.

In the autumn of 1832 he was invited to take the chair of Sacred Rhetoric in the Theological Seminary at Andover. For some time he had been thought of for this important post. He was already widely known and greatly admired in New England. He had received his doctorate of divinity from Williams College in 1826. Many of his summer vacations had been spent in New Haven, where he was on terms of affectionate intimacy with Drs. Taylor, Fitch, Goodrich, and Bacon, and where he often preached with extraordinary power; while his recent pastorate in Boston, brief though it was, had left a strong impression in that region. He had just delivered the annual address before the Porter Rhetorical Society—one of his most eloquent productions. It was not strange, therefore, that soon after his return to Philadelphia a call reached him from Andover, accompanied with very urgent persuasions from the professors and the students. After a good deal of hesitation he declined it.

"A very remarkable letter from Prof. Stuart, full of the noblest feeling and surpassingly eloquent, and one also from the students, urged me to review my decision. A review of it, but for one cause, probably, would not have changed it. My labors, the happiest of my life, had impaired my health."

He was suffering, in fact, from a serious disease, and his physician, Dr. Physic, advised him strongly to make the change, warning him that he could not long continue his labors in Philadelphia. Under the pressure of this consideration, he decided to go to Andover. But to the close of his days it remained with him a question whether he had decided wisely; indeed, he inclined to think it would have been better for him to have stayed among his own people. In a review of his Philadelphia ministry, written in 1865, he assigns strong reasons in favor of this view. But I venture to think he was quite mistaken; and that even had his health allowed him to remain, it was better for him to leave. It seems to me clear that God had a special work for him to do, which could have been done nowhere else than in New York. But the truth is, his whole heart clave to Philadelphia. His work there was to him, he says, as heaven upon earth; his people almost idolized him; he and they were one; and what scenes of refreshing from the presence of the Lord they had passed through together! No wonder he ever after looked back to those halcyon days with such yearning and delight; or that, whenever he walked again the streets of Philadelphia, an unusual buoyancy marked his steps.*

He entered upon his work at Andover with charac-

---

* While this discourse is passing through the press, I have received a graphic account of Dr. Skinner's ministry in Philadelphia from one of his oldest and most esteemed friends in that city, Mr. Joseph H. Dulles. It will be found in Appendix B.

teristic zeal and singleness of mind; but soon found out that it was very different work from preaching the gospel.

"What a novice in teaching Sacred Rhetoric! It is a harder business, in comparison, than teaching in either of the other departments. Dr. Griffin returned from it to preaching again after a short trial. Dr. Porter did well in it, in some respects; but it was to him very onerous; he died before his time. I think it was he who said, that it was easier to find a hundred men to fill the theological chair, than one for that of Homiletics. It was a new business in the American church. Theology had been nearly all in all in sacred education. Homiletics had no place in it."

Dr. Skinner labored hard, at Andover and, afterwards, in our own Seminary, to raise this study to its proper place. Drawing from the rich stores of his own experience, he applied the art of preaching to sermons on the chief topics of theology, and showed how they should be treated in the pulpit. In this way he himself taught theology as well as Homiletics, and asserted his right to do so with earnestness and decision. He magnified his office as one of unsurpassed dignity and importance in the training of effective ministers of the gospel.

But lecturing at the Seminary was not his only occupation at Andover. Besides preaching in his turn in the chapel, he preached frequently on Sabbath-evening to the two academies, in which were some four hundred young persons, of both sexes. In the pulpit of the North parish, in those of Boston, Newburyport, and other places, his voice was often heard. Preaching was still his greatest delight; and wherever he went crowds came together to hear him. He took especial pleasure in assisting at "protracted meetings," and his sermons on such occasions were pungent and effective in the highest degree.

A PROTRACTED MEETING.

Let me give his own account of one of these meetings. It was at Newburyport. The Presbyterian and Orthodox Congregational churches were united in it.

"A work of God so powerful and so extensive through a whole population, I have seen in no place. The Unitarians and Episcopalians did not oppose it. Its subject was the town; revival was the rule, indifference was exceptional, and the exception was unnoticed. Every interest was displaced, or subordinated, by interest in religion. . . . Newburyport (Whitefield's monument was here) was full of God's special presence. How awful was this place! The meeting ended on a Sabbath-evening. I have not seen a parallel occasion. There was a general convocation in the Rev. Mr. Milton's church, the largest in the town. A special arrangement was made to accommodate male attendants. They occupied the pews below; females sat in the gallery. I never saw so interesting a mass of men. They were of middle age, very vigorous, healthful, masculine, intelligent; as closely packed as possible; not less in number, it was supposed, than a thousand. The large gallery contained nearly as many women. All the ministers were present. After sermon, Dr. Dimmick said to me : ' I wish you would repeat here what was done at the Andover protracted meeting.' ' I am ready but cannot proceed without the consent of the other ministers (the venerable Dr. Dana was one of them).' 'They cannot refuse in the circumstances.' He consulted them ; they promptly concurred. I then made, for substance, the following address to the solemn assembly :

"'We have been, for several days considering with unusual seriousness and care, the great concern of our eternity. The subject is now in our thoughts more distinctly and completely, than it was; and, probably, than it will ever be in this world. This very evening we have been weighing it in the balance of judgment very particularly and carefully (*Counting the cost.* Luke xiv. 28-32, was my theme). It is probable that very many of you have impressions of it juster and deeper than you have heretofore felt. Would it not be well if you should to-night, ere you return to your homes, determinedly decide in accordance with these impressions? If you should depart without deciding, will you be likely to decide at all, or, if you do, to decide as truly, as you will, if you decide here and now? Will you have, at any other moment, equal advantages for deciding aright? You are greatly moved, it may be ; but you must be so moved when the decision is made, if it be a right one. The opposing influences of sin, the world, and Satan, cannot be overcome, but by the strongest counter influences. It is not these latter influences, but the others, that are likely to be too strong. Get away from the holy, heavenly influences under which we are now sitting, and think ye, that ye will have better advantages for exercising judgment and discretion in reference to the infinite interests of your immortality. Will worldly business or society, will your families, will your closets, even, offer you a better chance for right action in this case, than this holy place, filled as it is with the gracious presence of God? It is, therefore, proposed to you, that you make the prayer about to be offered, an expression of a deliberate in-wrought determination to be henceforth, by the grace of God, followers of Christ. And if you accept this proposal, to indicate that you do, by standing up, by yourselves, when the prayer is offered. Those of you, who have already made a religious profession, or who do not accept the proposal, not being willing to commit yourselves to-night to the obligations and relations of a Christian life, are requested to remain sitting; that the others may be distinguished from you.'

"When the usual, *Let us pray*, was spoken, the scene was a more imposing one than any other assembly I ever saw presented. Hardly less than five hundred large men, and nearly, or quite, as many women, were instantly on their feet. I have never heard that 'the measure,' in this instance, was objected to by any one. The circumstances and the result were its justification. It has been reported that, as the fruit of this protracted meeting, about one thousand persons were received into the churches of Newburyport and that neighborhood; and that very few of them have failed to maintain a Christian character."

PASTOR OF THE MERCER STREET PRESBYTERIAN
CHURCH, NEW YORK.

In the year 1835, a number of Christian people,

connected with the Laight street, the Bleecker street, and other Presbyterian congregations in this city, determined to form a new church and erect a new edifice up-town. They applied to Dr. Skinner to take charge of the movement. He consented to do so. The church was organized October 25, 1835, and on the 8th of November he was installed as its pastor. For six months divine service was held in the chapel of the University. In the spring of 1836, the pleasant house of worship in Mercer street was finished and dedicated to God. And here commenced Dr. Skinner's last, and, in some respects, most important pastorate. He was not unwilling to leave Andover. The duties of his professorship he had discharged with eminent fidelity and success; but they were somewhat irksome to him. He was in the full vigor of intellectual manhood; his health was restored; and the pulpit was still his throne. He loved to preach as he loved no other work. The call to New York was very strong and attractive. Some of the leading members of the Presbyterian church in the city, were enlisted in the new movement. If he was ever to return to the pastoral life, now was his opportunity. He never regretted the change. And as we look back to it, and consider what interests were involved, we cannot doubt that, in making it, he acted most wisely and in full accordance with the will of God. What other man, then living, could have taken his place and done his work in this city? The great schism in the

Presbyterian church was soon to occur. The Union Theological Seminary was about to be founded. Dr. Skinner's history, his uncommon weight of personal and ministerial character, his wide acquaintance and intimacy with leading men in New England and the Middle States, and his position as the pastor of one of the strongest metropolitan churches, gave him an influence in the New School body, and in sustaining as well as shaping the course of the Union Seminary, which nobody else could have wielded.

I have time barely to touch upon his thirteen years in the Mercer street church. They were years of most faithful, unwearied and successful labor. Something of his youthful fire in the pulpit, something of his old popularity, was, no doubt, wanting. But what ripeness of Christian experience, what clear insight into divine things, what scriptural and theological power, what rousing appeals to both the natural and the regenerate man, what holy unction, particularly in seasons of special interest and revival marked his preaching! With what almost inspired fervors of soul he led the devotions of the sanctuary! How he fed the people of God with the finest of the wheat! The characteristic features of his own religious life and temper—deep spirituality, reverence for God and sympathy with God in His demands upon man, a profound feeling of the reality and infinite evil of sin, passionate desire of holiness; an adoring sense of the glory of Christ, of the saving virtue of His sacrifice of

Himself upon the cross, and of the blessedness of vital union with Him by faith; high views respecting the entire consecration of person, time, talent, property, everything, to the service of the Master, by every one of His disciples; a conviction that the man, who has made up his mind to take right views of sin, has made up his mind to go through this world very much alone; joy in the Lord, and exulting assurance of the coming triumphs of His kingdom;—these all were equally marked characteristics of his ministry in the Mercer street church.

He was aided in his work by a noble band of elders and brethren. Few churches in the land combined so much intelligence, maturity and weight of character, earnest piety, public spirit, catholicity, and large-hearted pecuniary liberality, with so much attractive social and domestic culture, as the Mercer street Presbyterian church, during the first thirteen years of its existence. What honored names—Markoe, Mason, Shipman, Phelps, father and son, Bull, Boorman, Butler, Wilder, De Forest, Wainwright, Lockwood, Noyes, Haines, Blatchford, Coit, and others like them—not to speak of the living—adorn its history.

"It was a people (to use his own language) as worthy of the best type of pastoral labor as any one I have known. I felt it to be so. The sense of my responsibility was more than I could endure. My health failed under the severe pressure of my duties. Another sphere awaited me. I was again professor in a theological school."

PROFESSOR IN THE UNION THEOLOGICAL SEMINARY.

We come now to the closing period of his public life. He resigned his pastoral charge February 17, 1848; and in March of the same year, was inaugurated Professor of Sacred Rhetoric, Pastoral Theology and Church Government, in the Union Theological Seminary in this city. Here he labored without interruption for well-nigh a quarter of a century. He was fifty-seven years old on taking the chair; he was almost eighty years old when he left it for his seat in glory. His appointment was one of singular fitness. As a Director of the Institution, he had from the first been identified with its history, and felt the deepest interest in its prosperity. But for his powerful aid and that of his church, it would probably either have had no existence, or would have perished in its infancy. The position to which he was called required the highest type of personal and Christian character, large pastoral experience, a thorough acquaintance with the art of preaching and the care of souls, the best literary and theological culture, in union with generous sympathies and an unfailing spirit of brotherly kindness and charity in dealing with the doubts, the trials, and the imperfections, of young men preparing for the sacred office. Dr. Skinner possessed all these qualifications in a very unusual degree. For a third of a century he had been one of the first preachers and sacred orators in the land; as a pastor and guide of souls he had few equals; he was an accomplished scholar, enthusiastic in the pursuit and discussion of theological truth, and able to excite similar enthusiasm in others; his piety was full of spiritual depth and unction; and he was a model of the Christian gentleman. He had, moreover, discharged the duties of this very chair, for several years, in the leading seminary of New England, besides having written and published a number of admirable essays on subjects connected with it.

I will not attempt now a review of his labors, or a full estimate of what he accomplished, in the service of the Union Theological Seminary. That will be done, in due time, I trust, by one of his colleagues, or by one of his old pupils. He brought to his new task, as we have seen, rare gifts; and he devoted all of them to it without stint. He was as faithful, diligent, and *totus in illis*, in the theological chair, as he had ever been in the pulpit. He began at once a thorough course of study on the different branches of his professorship. The fruit of his industry soon appeared in Vinet's "Pastoral Theology," and "Homiletics," translated and edited by him with excellent taste and skill. Had he done nothing else than to give these two precious works to the Christian public, he would have rendered his department an invaluable service. He prepared his lectures with the utmost care, and continued to re-write and improve them to the last. His intercourse with his pupils, both in and out of the class-room, was not merely that of a teacher; it was also the fellowship of a friend and brother in Christ. He invited them, one by one, to visit him at his home; he manifested an affectionate personal interest in their fortunes; he sympathized tenderly with them in their mental struggles, cheered them in their despondency, was very patient and considerate towards their faults, and helped them by his prayers and with the lessons of his own experience, to get the victory over their religious doubts and perplexities. For this how many of them, now scattered far and wide through the earth, bless God at every remembrance of him!* And in years to come, when the Union Theological Seminary, transplanted to the neighboring height, now waiting to be adorned by it, and thence shedding light and blessing over all lands, shall recount God's favors to it, *this* will be reckoned, I do not doubt, one of the most signal—that, for nearly a quarter of a century, it enjoyed the instructions, the friendship, and the prayers, of THOMAS H. SKINNER as one of its professors!

INCIDENTS OF TRAVEL.

Dr. Skinner's life was passed chiefly in his study and in absorbing devotion to the practical duties of his calling. He had little fondness for travel, or for any business that took him away from home. His journeying was confined mostly to an annual visit to

---

* In Appendix C will be found two striking testimonies on this point from old pupils of Dr. Skinner.

the scenes of his boyhood in North Carolina, to an occasional attendance upon the sessions of the General Assembly, and to two visits to the Old World. He first crossed the Atlantic in 1839. It was next to martyrdom for him to go; but ill-health and the entreaty of friends at length prevailed, and he took passage in the *Great Western*. His first Sabbath in England was spent at Bristol. At the close of worship, he relates that he was accosted by a person of gentlemanly appearance, who, hearing that he had just arrived from America, inquired of him, if he was acquainted with "the great Dr. Channing?" The conversation led him to refer to another, and, as he thought, still greater man, then living near Bristol. "Who?" "Mr. John Foster, of Stapleton." The gentleman had never heard of such a man! Dr. Skinner shortly after visited Mr. Foster, was very kindly received, and left him with a deepened impression of his worth and greatness. From Bristol he proceeded to London, thence across the channel to Germany, then back to London through Belgium, and from London to Edinburgh, where he had the pleasure of meeting Dr. Chalmers.

"Received by him with the utmost cordiality and sweetness of manner. Was as free in the company of this great man as if I had been an equal. Walked with him through the Botanical Gardens. He wanted me to admire a fine panorama of the city and its environs; but my admiration was so absorbed in the man, that I could hardly notice anything else. An inexpressible beauty in the character of Dr. Chalmers. . . . . Dr. C., very unlike Foster, but quite as simple in manner. How happy to have 'laid eyes' on two such men! Cathedrals, scenery, all sights and spectacles—how vapid, compared with these specimens of intellectual and spiritual excellence! In all England and Scotland there is not, *me judice*, the like of them."

He returned home in the autumn in the *British Queen*, narrowly escaping shipwreck on the passage. In 1846, I believe, he crossed the sea again, and assisted at the formation of the Evangelical Alliance in London.

For many years before his death he was accustomed to pass his summers at Newport, R. I. The spot became so much endeared to him that, on resigning his chair in the seminary—as he had intended to do this spring—he meditated making it a home for the rest of his days. Dr. Channing, though born and brought up there, can hardly have loved Newport more. He passed much of his time in reading and study, enlivened by intercourse with old friends, and, occasionally, by a fishing excursion, which revived the memories of his boyhood on the pleasant shores of Albemarle Sound. He also took a lively interest in the church, whose services he attended, and at whose weekly evening-meeting his voice was often heard in prayer and exhortation.*

* See in Appendix A, an extract from a sermon by its pastor, the Rev. Dr. Thayer, preached shortly after his death.

THE TIMES HE LIVED IN.

In reviewing the character of Dr. Skinner, a glance at the times in which his lot was cast, will aid us greatly. The nearly three score-years, covered by his ministry and teaching, form one of the most wonderful periods in secular history, and one no less remarkable in the history of the Church. In some of its aspects there is nothing else like it in the annals of the race. It was marked by extraordinary revivals of religion. It was a new era of missionary zeal and evangelism at home and abroad. Our theological seminary—now one of the grand educational institutions of American Christianity—belongs to this period. More Bibles have been circulated during these sixty years, many times over, than in all previous ages. Nearly the whole globe has been opened, for the first time, to the preaching of the Gospel. What amazing events and changes in the social and secular spheres have come to pass since 1812, I need not stop to tell you. And if there were any three points on the continent where the best and strongest religious forces of this marvelous epoch were concentrated, they were Philadelphia, that old haunt of Presbyterianism, Andover, which may be taken as representing New England, and this cosmopolitan city of New York. At these three central points Dr. Skinner spent the whole of his public life. Nor did he merely feel the full influence of the dominant religious forces; he was himself one of them. He took part in the new movements with his whole mind and soul and strength. And thus the spirit of the age and his own spirit were continually acting and reacting upon each other. Although a man of strong individuality, full of fresh, original traits, he was also a man of singular intellectual susceptibility and power to absorb the good with which he came in contact, whether in books or in real life. The ruling sentiments, the benevolent aims, and the bright hopes of the new era, that so many thought was to usher in the millennial glory, were wrought into his spiritual consciousness and inspired his whole career. One of his old friends and parishioners, the late Hon. Benjamin F. Butler—an admirable judge—said to me once, that Dr. Skinner reminded him of the canonized saints and fathers of the Church; and for fervent piety, devotion, and knowledge of divine things, he deserved well to be ranked among that illustrious and goodly company; but still he was a true representative of his own age—a child not of the third, or the twelfth, or the sixteenth, but of the nineteenth century.

Among his most intimate friends and co-laborers, at different periods of his ministry, were such men as Dr. James P. Wilson, Rev. James Patterson, Dr. Lyman Beecher, Moses Stuart, and Albert Barnes,—men who made a profound impression upon him, as they did upon their generation. He tenderly cherished their memories and always spoke of them in terms of affectionate and grateful admiration.

HIS FAVORITE AUTHORS.

And this suggests a word about his favorite authors. They were the old Puritan divines of the seventeenth century—Owen, Baxter, Flavel, John Howe—Thomas à Kempis and Archbishop Leighton,* Pascal, and President Edwards; and among recent writers, above all others, John Foster, Isaac Taylor, and Vinet. He regarded Howe as a very prince of divines. Of the treatise on the Trinity by that great nonconformist, he not long since spoke to me as, in his view, unequaled. But his reading was by no means confined to these authors. His library contained not only the great masters of English and American religious thought, but the great masters in philosophy, poetry and general literature as well. In a conversation with him not long before his death, he spoke of the lively pleasure he had received from reading some portions of Mr. Emerson's "Society and Solitude." He had a catholic taste and delighted himself exceedingly in all good books, whether old or new. Indeed, his mind

---

* The following passage occurs in his note-book, under the date July 9, 1866:

"The eye of a godly man is not fixed on the false sparkling of the world's pomp, honor and wealth; it is dead to them, being quite dazzled with a greater beauty. The grass looks fine in the morning, when it is set with those liquid pearls, the drops of dew that shine upon it, but if you can look but a little while on the body of the Sun, and then look down again, the eye is as it were dead; it sees not this faint shining on the earth that it thought so gay before; and as the eye is blinded and dies to it, so within a few hours, that gaiety quite evanishes and dies of itself."—LEIGHTON, 1 Pet. ii. 24.

Next to the inspired books, I must place this work of Leighton's; and I think that in his remarks on this 24th verse of Chapter II. he transcends himself.

was so open and hospitable to new thoughts, that he was quite inclined to esteem them the best it had ever known or entertained.

HIS THEOLOGY.

Of his theological position and views, I need add but little to what has been said already. He commenced his ministry at a time when religious life and opinion were about to assume new types and to develop themselves with vehement force; and such times are apt to be marked by more or less of misunderstanding, strife and division. Dr. Skinner belonged to what became known as New School; he was in full sympathy with that side; and he avowed his convictions without fear or favor. But no candid person can read his writings, as none could have heard him preach, without perceiving that he was a sound, earnest, highly evangelical and orthodox divine of the Calvinistic type. He himself was very far from feeling that the New School were all right or the Old School all wrong. His mature judgment was—not to speak now of mere questions of ecclesiastical policy—that while both schools agreed in being truly Calvinistic, and both alike sincerely adopted the Westminster Confession of Faith as containing the system of doctrine taught in the Holy Scriptures, the points in which they really differed were of minor consequence, and concerned not the vital substance of the Gospel, but only the best modes of viewing, stating and explaining certain of its dogmatic truths. He believed in progress of religious thought, and loved to quote the pithy saying of Dr. Owen: "Let new light be derided whilst men please; he will never serve the will of God in his generation, who sees not beyond the line of foregoing ages." But believing also in the divine authority and fullness of "the faith once delivered to the saints," he had no notion that it needed to be completed or could be improved by modern thought. Theological science would, no doubt, continue to advance with the advancing knowledge and experience of the Church; but Christianity itself, as a revelation of God's will and a way of salvation, was and had been from the beginning perfect and entire, wanting nothing. He was, therefore, both conservative and liberal; conservative in holding fast to the old apostolic doctrine, as taught in the Holy Scriptures; liberal in striving and in bidding others strive to attain a more complete and practical understanding of it.*

HIS THEORY OF PREACHING.

His theory of preaching was very high and was in harmony with his theory of Christian truth. It was all summed up in the address on "Preaching Christ," delivered from this pulpit to the graduating class of the Seminary three years ago. Who that was present can have forgotten the opening sentence of that address?

---

* Some excellent remarks on this subject may be found in his discourse entitled "The Old in the New," delivered by him as the retiring Moderator of the General Assembly, in St. Louis, May 17, 1855.

"I feel that it becomes me to be considerate as to what I should say to you now, probably the last time I shall speak on an occasion like the present. Aware of my close proximity to the end of my course, I would fain place myself there, and speak as I shall wish I had done if the ear were never to hear my voice again. How unsuitable to my position and age were an utterance from my lips now such as man's vanity or 'man's wisdom' teacheth!"

PREACH CHRIST; PREACH OF THE ABILITY WHICH THE HOLY SPIRIT GIVETH; PREACH THUS TO THE UTMOST OF YOUR STRENGTH.

These maxims, or precepts, contain the vital essence of his homiletics; and he unfolds and enforces them, in this address, in a manner truly apostolic. He laid the utmost stress upon making Christ's sacrifice of Himself the chief element in preaching Him.

"The immediate intendment of this preaching is a *reproduction of Christ as an atoning Saviour in the consciousness of the hearers;* to effect which it strives to 'set Him forth' as 'before their eyes,' 'crucified,' hanging on the accursed tree, bearing there our sins in His own immaculate body. Preaching Christ is successful with reference to its proximate purpose, in proportion as it succeeds in this endeavor. Paul tells the Galatians, (iii. 1,) that such was his success as a preacher to them in this respect, that the scene of the crucifixion was, in effect, vividly re-enacted in their very presence. This is what the preaching of Christ aspires to, and what it achieves when it gains its direct end, as a suasory or rhetorical effort. Evangelical preaching, in its just idea, is a divine ordinance for giving, as perfectly as possible, a life-presence to the transaction of Christ's immolation, under Pontius Pilate, 'at the place of a skull,' outside of the city of Jerusalem; for giving this tragical transaction universality; for making it, in effect, to all mankind, everywhere, and to the end of the world, a living reality, as taking place in their presence—a reality the greatest that ever came or ever will come to pass.

"Such, then, my dear brethren, must be the manner of your preaching, if you would have it true to the purpose of its institution. It implies no restriction as to particular subjects. It only demands that whatever subject you treat, your sermon on it be filled, as completely as possible, with Christ as suffering the death of the cross to atone for the sins of the world; that you make Christ, in this view of His passion, the essence and life, the '*succus et sanguis*' of your entire ministry; that you make the great atonement pulsate through the whole and each particular instance of your preaching, as the heart of a vigorous body pulsates through all its members and fibres."

In applying the second maxim, he uses this impressive language:

"Be out of communion with the Holy Spirit in preaching; be without his coöperation in it, and what will be its character before Him who understands it, and whom alone it supremely concerns you to please? Think of the peculiarity of the business of preaching: were it but a common operation of spiritual life, you could perform it only as aided by the Holy Spirit. No man can say that Jesus is the Lord, but by the Holy Ghost. But this singular work of public preaching:—What is done on earth, might I not say, in heaven, of higher spirituality? It is not merely human, it is strictly divine-human work; work impossible even to the apostles before they received the illapse of the Holy Ghost! Nay, we are told expressly that our Lord himself received the Holy Ghost to qualify him for preaching the Gospel. Preaching, speaking as God's mouth, the infinite things of the Spirit; so speaking, with discernment, with feeling, with words, and with delivery, suited to the nature and purpose of the business; can you wonder that the mightiest of the reformers, even when near the end of his course, never ascended the pulpit '*sine tremore?*' Nay, can you be surprised that even Paul confessed himself to have been agitated 'with fear, and much trembling,' in his ministry among the Corinthians? (1 Cor. ii. 3.) But, if you would fulfill the former precept, take heed to the present one, and you will, you cannot but attain your end. You will, of necessity, preach Christ, if you preach with the Spirit's help. He gives no aid, no countenance, in preaching aught else. Christ is the Holy Spirit's only theme, To show Christ, to glorify Christ, is his mission in the world. In preaching, especially, the chief part of which belongs to him, this is his only aim. Preach, then, without preaching Christ, and what is it that you do? You are about some business of your own, not what the Spirit is intent upon. If he is in any manner with you, it is not to produce through you a specimen of true preaching; you make discourse simply natural, not spiritual; it is only a *human*, not a divine-human production. He may be very intellectual, very eloquent, very admirable; the Spirit may in some way serve himself of it. His doing so does not change its character, or imply his approbation of it. He is not pleased with it; he certainly is not pleased with *you;* he does not bless you—your praise is of men, not of him: you have your reward."

In enforcing his third maxim, he says:

"The main reason for this precept is that it is only by observing it that you can carry out to completion the two former ones. Only by such diligence applied to preaching Christ through divine aid, can you make full proof of your ministry. And this reason will prevail with you, so far as the force of consistency or congruity prevails. In the first place you cannot but observe it, if you obey the precept I have been just enforcing—if you are led by the Holy Spirit in your ministry—for the earnestness of the Spirit in this business is unmitigated. What must be the intensity of your working if it coincides with that of the Spirit of God? His zeal in the work is like the zeal of Christ, of which it is written that it consumed him, 'ate him up.' And it never abates; it is as an ever-burning flame of fire. It varies in its applications; it is sometimes seemingly latent and even regressive; it has apparent rests and cessations, but even in these its energy is unrestrained, its proper temper is still as 'the melting fire when it burneth.' Correspondently, your preaching must needs vary in its particular instances and seasons, but it will not vary in its inherent temper if it continue in keeping with the temper of the Holy Spirit's activity, and it ought, as far as possible, to do so. 'Whereunto I also labor,' says Paul, 'striving according to his working which worketh in me mightily.' Keep yourself, then, according to your measure, in coöperation with the Holy Spirit in preaching. Take him as your antecedent and prompter in the business, and think what must be the general type of your ministry? Among ministers, to whom will you willingly give precedence in energy of determination, in necessity and urgency of action? To Edwards or Brainerd, or Whitfield or Baxter, or any other model preacher? Will your mark of aspiration be lower than that of St. Paul?

"But, again, the Spirit's tone of working apart, will the *proper preaching impulses*, the motive forces which have play in the work, permit any voluntary short-coming or slackness in your ministry? What are these motives? One of them is love for the perishing souls of men, preaching being the chief means of their salvation. How impossible to be really actuated by this love, without being, for the time, absorbed by it? The whole world is without value compared with the value of a human soul. Consider that the actual salvation of the meanest soul of man gives cause for new joy to the angels of God; consider that there was no ransom for such a soul less costly than the Great Redeemer's precious blood. How inconceivable, that one should be intelligently in earnest in seeking to save immortal souls, without putting himself into his effort wholly and absolutely. And your life-work, remember, is as one such effort prolonged to the end of your course. You are consecrated to saving men by your vocation and ordination as preachers. Were this the only impulse to diligence, might it not be well asked: 'What man on earth is so pernicious a drone as an idle clergyman?' But there is a mightier impulse; not *your* love of souls, but *a sense in you of the immeasurable love which Christ had for them*. This motive had such force in the ministry of Paul—a model to you, my brethren—that it caused him to be thought beside himself, (2 Cor. v. 13.) Was it excessive in this great example? There remains a motive greater yet than this, one including the two former, but of far wider scope than either of these, namely, a *sense of the surpassing glory of the redemptive scheme*, or of the glory of God as thereby displayed, glory transcending that of all other Divine works, whether of creation or providence. Be but touched, my young brethren, with a sense of this glory, (and why should you not, like Paul, like Whitfield, live continually in its blaze?) and what will be able to restrain or impair your energy as preachers?"

I have quoted these passages for a twofold reason, because they contain the result of Dr. Skinner's lifelong thought and study on the great subject of preaching, and because they afford, also, a much more faithful picture than any words of mine could give of his own ideal and practice, as a minister of the gospel.

HIS CATHOLIC SPIRIT AND DELIGHT IN REUNION.

I have spoken of his views of Christian truth and of the right way to preach it. His theory of Christian life and fellowship was in keeping with both. He abhorred all narrowness, bigotry and mere sectarian zeal. His whole course as a minister and theological teacher, and not less his early religious associations, led him to cherish the warmest sentiments of fraternal sympathy and affection for all who love our Lord Jesus Christ in sincerity. Episcopalians, Methodists, Baptists, and Dutch Reformed, were among his dearest friends. With Congregationalists his relations were especially close and cordial; indeed, for several years he had lived among them and been himself one of them. And although loyal and earnest in devotion to his own branch of the Presbyterian Church, some of his most cherished intimacies were with members of the other branch. I may mention the venerable Dr. Hodge, of Princeton, for whose expositions of the Inspired Word he often expressed his admiration, and between whom and himself there subsisted, for more than half a century, a most tender and devoted friendship.* He deemed it a matter of vital importance to the rapid progress and triumph of the Gospel, that all the true disciples of Christ, of whatever name, should be brought nearer together. When the movement toward Reunion commenced, he watched it with deep interest, gave it his approval, his counsels and his prayers, advocated it on the floor of the General Assembly, at Harrisburg, in a most impressive speech, and hailed its consummation with intense joy and thankfulness, as an event full of promise to the whole American church.

HIS PATRIOTISM.

It was the habit of his mind to take a large and liberal view of public events, both in the religious and the political sphere. Let any one read his sermon on "Love of Country," preached in December, 1850, a time of great party excitement; or his sermon on "Education and Evangelism," preached in October of

---

* See in Appendix A, a letter of Dr. Hodge to the Faculty of the Union Theological Seminary.

the same year, and he will be impressed with this fact. In the first-mentioned sermon he expresses himself on the subject of SLAVERY in the following manner:

"This is becoming a subject of extreme interest in this country. It is moving deeply our religious bodies, entering with great earnestness and with decisive effect into our political contests, and profoundly agitating our national councils. As Christian patriots, we cannot be justified in holding toward it the position of neutrality or indifference. It is not probable that the excitement which has been created will subside without some result of importance to the nation. What course does true patriotism require us to take in regard to it? Let no man content himself with denouncing the excitement as the fruit of fanatical zeal. That cannot be done indiscriminately without casting reproach on not a few of the most excellent and honored of our citizens, and also without disregard to historic truth. This movement in our nation, unhappily as it has proceeded in too many instances, is referable to a spirit in the age—an invincible spirit, we trust it will prove to be found—which seeks the universal emancipation of man, which should be resolved into the triumph of Christian truth as its remote cause, and which republican America, as having proclaimed to the world the natural equality of mankind from the beginning of her independence, cannot, without palpable inconsistency, resist. Slavery, as a system, should find advocates everywhere throughout the earth sooner than in this land of freedom. It should, and we hope soon will be, the universal desire that the institution utterly cease."

When, ten years later, the crisis arrived and the war of Secession burst upon our country, Dr. Skinner showed himself a Christian patriot of the highest order. Though himself a native of the South, and still bound to it by the tenderest ties, he did not hold back, or waver, for a moment; he spoke out, with a loud and clear voice, for the cause of the Union; he prayed for its success, as only he could pray; he hailed the Proclamation of Emancipation with warm approval; and when the mighty struggle ended in the triumph of the nation, and the overthrow of Slavery, he blessed God that he had lived to see the day!

Almost to the last hour of his life he read eagerly the public journals, and watched the course of events with as much interest as if he were just entering upon, instead of just leaving, the stage of earthly affairs. He fully sympathized with Germany in the late gigantic contest, and anticipated grand results to the cause of humanity and Christian truth from her splendid triumph. The results of the Vatican Council, whose proceedings he carefully followed, would also, he believed, though in a different way, turn out for the furtherance of truth and righteousness.

HIS DOMESTIC CHARACTER.

Of his domestic and social virtues, I would gladly speak at length. As son, brother, husband, father and friend, his life was crowned with beauty. Nobody knew him as he really was, who did not know him at the fireside. The relation which subsisted between his eldest brother and himself, as depicted by his own pen, is full of the very poetry of friendship.* He had an exquisite sense of character, and could portray it with the skill of a master. His portrait of Mrs. Lowther, "the loveliest, most beautiful, most interesting of women," as he calls her, is one of the finest things I know of in the language.† The genial glow and enthusiasm of his nature, which rose so high in his religious life, gave an exceedingly rich flavor also to his

---

* See "A Sketch of the Life and Character of the late Joseph B. Skinner. By his Brother, Thomas H. Skinner." For the account of Dr. Skinner's parents, birth-place, and other incidents, I am indebted to this interesting little volume. It should be here stated that, although his brother Joseph sharply opposed his giving up the bar for the pulpit, the alienation was of short continuance. It is due alike to the elder and the younger brother to quote the following passage from the Memoir: "But for his kindness I should not have been sent to college. Under his direction and at his expense, I prosecuted a course of preparation for the bar until near the time of my admission to it, when I tried his affection to the uttermost by what he could not but regard as a very sudden and rash refusal of his choice of a profession for me. Tempted strongly, by my disappointing thus his fondest and long-cherished hopes respecting me, to leave me to myself, after a season of intense displeasure from him, his former munificence returned to me, to forsake me no more till we were separated by his death. Wherever I have been, there have ever been with me decisive proofs of his thoughtful and constant affection. In my seasons of severe trial, I have always had the aid of his wise counsel and his effectual sympathy; and when my usefulness has been restricted by want of opportunity, his hands have been opened to provide the means of supply. For my favorable position in Philadelphia, the latter half of my course there, the seed-time of my ministry, I was mainly indebted, under the divine blessing, to his influence, his suggestive wisdom, and his purse. When in another city I was exhausted and faint from labor, he urged me to travel in Europe for my restoration to health, and put at my disposal the means of compliance with his plan. He has always been afflicted in my affliction, and happy in making me and my household happy. And this tribute from me may be taken as an indication of what he was substantially to his other relations."—pp. 49, 50.

† See Appendix D.

earthly affections. You could not sit at his table, talk with him at his fireside or on his doorsteps, or meet him casually at the corner of the street, without feeling its sweet attraction. I have passed many, many happy hours with him; but none happier, or whose memory is more fragrant, than those spent in his own house, with his wife and children and grandchildren about him. Outside of his own immediate family, he had a wide circle of friends, both old and young, in New York, Philadelphia, and elsewhere, with whom, as time and opportunity permitted, he kept up to the last an affectionate intercourse. How they will henceforth miss his wonted visits! A young lady, to whom he had greatly endeared himself by his spiritual counsels and kind sympathy, wrote to me shortly after his death: "I miss him so terribly! I try not to dwell on him, yet sometimes in the night I awake with a burst of tears, as he comes visibly before me even in sleep." On last New-Year's day he started early and called upon an unusual number of his old friends. If the households, that were blessed on that day with his presence and godly conversation, had foreseen that in a single month he would be in heaven, they could hardly have been more vividly conscious of the privilege they were enjoying. He had just come from a union morning prayer-meeting, and his face still shone, while his heart seemed to be running over with devout, grateful and tender emotions. His closing years were, indeed, the ideal of a Christian old age;

full of patriarchal benignity, gentleness, sympathy and love.

HIS MENTAL AND PERSONAL TRAITS.

The leading features of his mental character have, perhaps, appeared sufficiently in the preceding narrative. The natural bent of his mind was reflective and logical, rather than imaginative. He speaks of having become conscious, early in his college course, that he had a gift for mathematics and for the investigation of abstract truth; and to the end of life he delighted in books and studies which required the most strenuous exercise of pure intellect. If this tendency had not been modified and counterbalanced by the depth and fervor of his convictions, he would never have been the powerful preacher that he was; indeed, in the later years of his ministry his sermons suffered, perhaps, some disadvantage from a too predominant intellectual tone. The profound and discriminating analysis, which renders them so instructive in the reading, detracted somewhat, doubtless, from their popular effect in the hearing. But in the earlier periods of his ministry this was far from being the case. If his preaching even in those days was unmarked by any special power of illustration or play of fancy, it glowed with a spiritual fire and energy of soul, which fused into one his most elaborate expositions of Christian doctrine, with all his high-wrought arguments and appeals, bringing them home to the conscience and heart of his hearers as a veritable message from God! For intellectual vigor and discrimination, combined with impassioned spiritual convictions, and the best results of scriptural and theological study and reflection, I suppose very few preachers of his generation could compare with Dr. Skinner.

Let me now speak of his more private and personal traits. In his character nature and grace were united in the finest proportions. The same bright and lovely qualities which in boyhood and youth so endeared him to his elder brother and to the whole circle of his friends, rendered him so dear to us also, who knew him two or three-score years later.

"The child was father of the man."

Old age often borders upon second childhood; in his case it bordered close upon first childhood; the fresh, sweet dawn of the morning of his existence mingling with and beautifying its sober evening. He was simplicity itself; it was his nature. He seemed as unconscious of his own virtues, as if it had never crossed his mind that he *could* possess them. A more transparent, unsophisticated, guileless, single-eyed, naive human being I never saw. He shrank from things false, artful or double-minded, as a delicate girl shrinks from what is coarse and impure. The foundations of his character were laid deep in truth and uprightness. How unsuspicious, how frank and trustful and magnanimous he was! How untainted by the vanities and ambitions of the world! How absorbed in good thoughts and high endeavors! What Professor Tyndall says of Farraday, might be applied, almost word for word, to him:

"The life of his spirit and of his intellect was so full, that the things which most men strive after were absolutely indifferent to him. A favorite experiment of his own was representative of himself. He loved to show that water in crystalizing, excluded all foreign ingredients, however intimately they might be mixed with it. Out of acids, alkalies, or saline solutions, the crystal came sweet and pure. By some such natural process in the formation of the man, beauty and nobleness coalesced, to the exclusion of everything vulgar and low. He did not learn his gentleness in the world, for he withdrew himself from its culture, and still the land of England contained no truer gentleman than he. Not half his greatness was incorporate in his science, for science could not reveal the bravery and delicacy of his heart."

I have spoken of his artless simplicity and self-unconsciousness. Let me give an illustration of it. He called, two or three years ago, upon an old friend, who said to him: "Just as you came in my wife was reading something which, I think, would interest you. Shall she read it again?" "Certainly. I shall be glad to hear it." It was a most eloquent and pathetic appeal for wrestling prayer, that God would give the Church more and better ministers. He listened intently, and when she had finished, expressed in the strongest terms his delight and approval. "Who is the author?" he asked. "It is from John Angell

James's 'Earnest Ministry.'" Whereupon he uttered a fervid eulogy upon that excellent man, and said the passage was well worthy of him. "But it is not by Mr. James; it is quoted." "From whom?" "From a book entitled, 'Religion of the Bible. Select Discourses, by Dr. Skinner, of New York.'"*

In his relations with his ministerial brethren, as in all the intercourse of life, he was the impersonation of generous and admiring sympathy. To his inbred courtesy, which showed him as one of nature's noblemen, grace superadded a holy sweetness and benignity that told of long and closest intimacy with the King of Glory. When in his higher moods, the smile upon his face, his friendly greeting, and the cordial grasp of his hand, wrought upon you with a kind of magnetic force; for hours afterwards you felt the happy influence, as if you had met an angel unawares. What shall I say of his freedom from envy, jealousy and like passions, which alas! sometimes steal even into the hearts of ministers of the Gospel. He seemed to take far more delight in the gifts and success of his ministerial brethren than his own. Mrs. Gillman once told me, that, during the nearly twenty years which Coleridge passed under her husband's roof at Highgate, she never heard him utter an angry word against the literary enemies who wrote malicious, bitter things about him; and such was his happy faculty of not seeing the faults and of

---

* I give the passage in Appendix E, not only for the sake of the anecdote, but as eminently adapted to the wants of the Church in our own day.

magnifying the virtues of his friends, that anybody he really loved was sure of his unbounded admiration. Something of the same characteristic belonged to Dr. Skinner. I know not that he had even a theological enemy; I never heard him speak of one; but how he loved to praise and magnify his friends. If one of them wrote an article, or a book, or preached a sermon that pleased him, in what admiring words he delighted to express his pleasure! There may have been at times a touch of weakness in it; but eminently great and good men are apt to have just such weaknesses.

HIS CHARACTER AS A HEARER.

The meek, childlike docility with which he received the word of life at the lips of his brethren, was most beautiful. I never had such a hearer, so punctual, attentive and considerate, so loving and devout. I never saw another quite like him. He drank in the simplest Christian truths, no matter how feebly uttered, almost as if they had been uttered by a man inspired. When, twenty years ago, I became the pastor of his old church in Mercer street, I was afraid of him among my hearers. There was not a man, woman or child in the congregation of whom I might not as well have been afraid. Never once during my seven years in his old church in Mercer street; never once during the ten years of my second pastoral relation to him, by word or look or action, did he cause me to feel that his sympathy was beginning to falter, or that he was not edified by my poor services. Nor did he fail to manifest his friendly interest. Some persons appear to think their minister scarcely more in need of expressions of their love and good will, while he is trying to lead them to heaven, than the locomotive that draws them over the iron track ; and they give about the same to the one as to the other. There are others who think that their minister stands in need of such expressions, in his place and degree, quite as truly as the husband needs them from the wife, or the parent from the child ; and they bestow them without stint. Dr. Skinner belonged to the latter class. He cherished a profound sense of the greatness, difficulties and peculiar trials of the minister's work, as also of the blessed privilege of hearing the word of life at his lips ; and he showed it by giving to his own pastor the aid and comfort of his constant, affectionate and grateful sympathy. But, after all, the most cheering help and support came from just seeing him in the sanctuary. His listening posture, his thoughtful, reverential aspect, the animated glance, the unconscious smile and nods of approval, when edified by the word preached, his closed eye and the rapt expression of his upturned face, as he stood and joined in singing the praises of his God and Saviour,—these made his very presence in church at once an open testimony for Christ, and a spiritual benediction alike to his minister and to the whole congregation.

HIS CHRISTIAN CHARACTER.

As a disciple of Jesus, Dr. Skinner attained heights seldom trodden in our day. Grace had penetrated every part and to the lowest depths of his being. The Christian life was to him an infinite reality. I have seen no truer type of its strength and beauty. His character was fashioned by no mere human power; it was, surely, the transcendent work of the Holy Ghost. He himself seemed not to have the faintest conception of its unearthly loveliness. His face, that shone so bright to others, was hidden from his own eye. *By the grace of God I am what I am!* That was the one thought which swallowed up and consecrated all others. Never did he appear so humble and tender and contrite in heart—so to hunger and thirst after righteousness, or to believe in the Lord Jesus Christ unto salvation with such absolute self-abandonment— as at the very time when the portals of glory everlasting were about to fly open for his ransomed spirit to pass through. He had made the long circuit of the Christian life, and was thus brought back again, enriched with the treasures of a great experience, to the unquestioning trust and childlike simplicity of its lowly beginning. One of his old and most intimate friends testified, on hearing of his death, " I thank God, on every remembrance of him, as the holiest man I have ever known." Certainly we may say, without any question, he was one of the holiest men of his generation. To use his own language respecting his bosom-friend Albert Barnes, we are "indebted to him, as a model minister, and preëminently as a model disciple of Christ." The doctrines which, for almost sixty years, he had so faithfully taught and preached to others, for sixty years wrought mightily in his own soul and reappeared at length, full-orbed, in his daily walk and conversation. His vigorous intellect, his resolute will, his ardent affections, with all the other powers of his strong and gifted nature, were fused and transfigured by their quickening influence. He was, in a word, a rare example of spiritual manhood, sound to the core, clear as a crystal, and reflecting in every lineament *the light of the knowledge of the glory of God shining in the face of Jesus Christ.*

But let no one imagine that he attained such heights of holiness without most laborious and devout culture; or that he was exempt from the struggles and trials of the Christian life. The grosser forms of temptation seemed hardly to touch him; but his intellectual and moral temperament rendered him, I think, peculiarly sensitive to those of a more refined, spiritual sort. Although a man of great faith, he had been subject at times to severe assaults of doubt; he knew what is meant by the "fiery darts of the adversary;" even to the last he had his dark, despondent moods. And this feature of his own experience qualified him to be such a tender and considerate counsellor of the young men who came to him with their religious difficulties and troubles of mind. The last Sabbath but one that he was ever at church, I preached a sermon on Faith as a gift of God. In the course of the sermon I quoted a striking passage from Richard Cecil's "Remains," in which he speaks of waking in pain at two o'clock in the morning and passing through a terrible conflict of soul. The passage seemed to make a strong impression upon Dr. Skinner. At the close of the service he met me on the pulpit stairs, took me by the hand, thanked me for my sermon, and, with deep feeling, said, "I fight *my* battles at two o'clock in the morning!" Several days afterwards he called and desired me to tell him where he could find the passage from Cecil. Let not those who are afflicted with fearful and skeptical thoughts, suppose that any strange thing has befallen them; some of the greatest and holiest servants of God, whose names adorn the annals of piety, have endured similar temptations.*

---

* The following is the passage referred to. Cecil is speaking of Belsham's answer to Wilberforce's "Practical Christianity:"

"I read it over while at Bath in the autumn of 1798. I waked in pain about two o'clock in the morning. I tried to cheer myself by an exercise of faith on Jesus Christ. I lifted up my heart to Him as sympathizing with me and engaged to support me. Many times have I thus obtained quiet and repose; but now I could lay no hold on Him; I had given the enemy an advantage over me; my habit had imbibed poison; my nerves trembled; my strength was gone: 'Jesus Christ sympathize with you and relieve you! It is all enthusiasm! It is idolatry! Jesus Christ has preached His sermons and done His duty and is gone to heaven; and there He is, as other good men are! Address your prayers to the Supreme Being.' I obtain relief in such cases by dismissing from my thoughts all that enemies, or friends, can say. I will have nothing to do with Belsham, or Wilberforce. I come to Christ Himself—I hear what He says—I turn over the Gospels—I need His conversations—I dwell especially on His farewell discourse with His disciples in St. John's Gospel. If there is meaning in words, and if Christ was not a deceiver, or deceived, the reality of the Christian life, in Him and from Him by faith, is written there as with a sunbeam."

HIS GIFT IN PRAYER.

He had an extraordinary gift in prayer. I have heard him in the pulpit and on great public occasions, when his devotional fervor, the energy and grasp of his petitions, and the soaring of his spirit, were truly wonderful. But it was in the little company gathered at the weekly evening service, or at the table of the Lord, that I have been most awe-struck by the power and unction of his prayers. Then I have heard him, as I never heard another mortal, plead and wrestle with the Most High, or pour out his soul in penitent confession, praise, thanksgivings, and adoring wonder, and thus soar aloft "with his singing robes about him," until it seemed as if he was just going to quit these lower regions forever!

For the following reminiscence I am indebted to my beloved brother, the Rev. Dr. Paxton, of this city:

"Being present last summer at the administration of the Lord's Supper in the church of the Rev. Dr. Thayer, in Newport, Dr. Skinner was called upon to make the opening prayer at the Communion Table. It was one of his favored moments, when, under an 'unction from the Holy One,' his mind was opened to a vivid apprehension of divine things, and his emotions were so stirred that he poured forth a strain of fervent devotion, such as made every one feel 'this is none other than the house of God and the gate of heaven.'

"He commenced with a personal address to the Saviour: 'O thou blessed Son of God, thou who art the

Only Begotten of the Father.' With these words his mind began to fire, and his heart to glow, and then followed a strain of adoring description, in which he gathered all the scriptural appellations and titles of our Lord into a resplendent diadem with which he crowned Him 'Lord of All.' The utterance of all this was in a peculiarly tender, but exultant tone, which wrought the audience into complete sympathy with himself, whilst he set before them such an attractive picture of the personal excellence and glory of our Lord, as made every one bow and adore.

"From this he passed to the crucifixion scene, upon which he dwelt in a most vivid detail, and thence to our Lord's exaltation. It was at this point he began to rise upon eagle pinions. Absorbed with the fresh apprehension which he seemed just then to receive of the Saviour's exaltation and preëminence in the heavenly kingdom, he dwelt upon the thought with exultation, rising higher and higher, both in his thought and utterance, until he seemed to forget himself in a transporting apprehension of things unseen and eternal.

"But the touching and melting part of the prayer was the conclusion, in which he set forth the benefits of the Saviour's death as they are represented in the Supper; and then, blending the Sacramental Supper with the marriage supper of the Lamb, he seemed to lift the whole scene, table, audience and all, to the Third Heavens, where he encircled it with glory and canopied it with light; seated the Master at the Table, and, gathering in the Angels and the Spirits of the Just made perfect, he made the whole scene pass in such vivid array, that when he suddenly concluded, I felt myself breathing a sigh of regret that I had so soon exchanged heaven for earth. The vivid impression of that prayer follows me to the present hour, and I never after met Dr. Skinner without feeling a sacred awe of one who had already been in heaven, in faith and prayer, and who was now standing all ready, with his spirit plumed for everlasting flight."*

His power in prayer was not more remarkable than his faith and delight in prayer. He not only went often and stayed long at the throne of grace himself, but he sought eagerly the intercession of his friends; entering into covenant with some of them that they should pray for each other daily.

"I began to love dear Dr. Skinner," (writes, after his death, an old friend in Boston, a layman well known for his Christian zeal and culture,) "when I began to know him—as a mere youth might know and love such a man—when he was my father's guest and honored pastor, for a

---

* I find the following allusion to Dr. Skinner at the close of Dr. Bushnell's striking article on "Prayer as related to God's Will," in *The Advance*, of June 29:

"I remember at this point with reverence, how fresh and refreshing were the prayers of our venerated friend and saintly brother, T. H. Skinner, just now taken from us. He was never satisfied with the rotundities of mere self-magnetizing worship. He was sinner enough and poor enough to want something and be making suit for it. And he was dealing visibly always with the will of God, making his confessions not as for tribute, and to pay the reverentials, but as for help. The scheme of his prayer, if I may use that term, was right, the taste of it was Christian. The very tones of it were in fact a prayer in themselves, and hearing them through an open window, not distinguishing the words, or knowing the man, almost any one would say, 'there is a man far in among God's purposes, not worshiping God as a wall, but as a Helper in the past and a Saviour in what is to come.' Indeed almost any one would get a better impression of Christ and deeper, from simply hearing one of this dear father's prayers, than from hearing any grandest sermon of salvation, or hosanna of praise."

brief time, at Pine street church. The opportunity to know and love him more was opened to me at Andover, in 1834. From that time until now he has been to me what no other man has ever been, or could be. When his last letter came—only a short week since—it prompted the thought of what it would be to be left in the world without his prayers. You may perhaps know, that, eleven years ago last August, he kindly asked me to enter into a covenant of mutual daily remembrance in prayer. From that day I have never failed to remember him at least twice daily; and in this last letter he speaks of his fulfillment of his part of the covenant."*

At the time of his conversion he was much aided

---

* The same friend writes a few days later:

"The last time I saw him, he repeated to me the beautiful and most Christian hymn beginning,

'My Jesus, as thou wilt,'

as expressive of his constant feeling. I have never seen, doubtless I never shall see, (to know him as being such,) so holy a man. I can never express my debt of gratitude to Him who gave me this friend of more than thirty-five years. Nor do I think I ever heard any preaching that had in it so much for me. This experience with him confirms me in the long-indulged conviction, that a friend can give us only what he *is*—not more. I once heard a clergyman asked, if he ever preached or prayed beyond his own experience? His reply was, 'If I did not, you would have very poor preaching.' I could not forbear saying, If you do preach beyond your own experience—and I would have added *pray*, as well, but that I think he waived that—we cannot fail to have poor preaching. Dr. Skinner certainly preached according to his aim and his unwearied endeavor, to be filled with all the fullness of the blessed God. I am sure his actual experience was much higher, broader, deeper, than his realized experience. I wish—without prejudice to the claims of any other—that his mantle might fall on me. Certainly he was clothed with the beauty of holiness. His sermons on Spiritual Religion, which have been more frequently appropriated without acknowledgment than probably any modern sermons, ought to be re-printed. There is nothing better in the language. And a host of sermons of his—especially those on the Beatitudes, ought to be added—not to that volume, but in other volumes, giving the religious public the advantage of his experience."

by the counsels of a pious negro. The name of this negro was Eden. He was a slave. He had been offered his freedom, but refused to accept it. He died in 1859. Dr. Skinner's tribute to this "sainted friend," as he called Eden, is touchingly beautiful. After describing his remarkable conversion and his eminently pious life, he proceeds thus:

"I was happy in my friendship with this humble man. It began early and was never suspended. At the time of his conversion he attended me as a servant; after it, I was accustomed to hear his voice in solitary prayer; and he was almost the only person to whom I could express my new feelings, when religion became my own supreme interest. Distance afterwards separated us, but did not diminish our friendship. We took pains to cherish and confirm it. By agreement, we daily (twice a day on the part of one of us, and, I doubt not, of the other, also, at least as often) remembered each other particularly in prayer. Twice he traveled several hundred miles by sea to visit me, and the anticipated pleasure of seeing him was always among the motives of my annual journeys to the South. We had short religious interviews when we met. Such were some of the means by which we kept our friendship advancing. Very pleasant to me, now that he is gone, is the reminiscence of them. Rather to be chosen than great riches, or great distinction in the world, was the interest I had in my friend Eden's prayers, of low estate though he was. The thousands of prayers, which I am sure he offered for me, with no feigned lips or unfeeling heart—how had I despised my mercies if his humble condition or aught else had made me lightly esteem these precious indications of his holy love."*

CONCLUSION.

But it is time to close; and yet I am loath to do so. To adopt his own words, in his delightful discourse on the death of his dear friend, Francis Markoe: "It gives a taste of heaven to hold communion with the idea of this most peculiar, Christ-like character. I am unwilling to let it be long out of my thought; it has not been long away from it, by day or night. I have found it very refreshing and sweet to me, to make this discourse upon it. My heart exults with great joy, in the hope of being united to this blest saint in the everlasting relations and employments of heaven."

For months before his departure, his friends began to feel that he was not long to remain on earth; there was a light in his face—a something in his whole tone and spirit—which told them so. He felt it himself, though, of course, for a very different reason. He had it in mind, again and again, to communicate to one of the directors of the Seminary his purpose to resign this spring; but did not "because (as he said to his family) it was some time till spring and he might still die at

---

* Soon after Eden's death, Dr, Skinner went South and preached a memorial discourse upon him to an overflowing house, composed largely of slaves. His text was Rev. i. 6, "Who hath made us kings and priests unto God." Subject—"The honor which Christianity puts upon man."

The tribute to Eden appeared in the *New York Observer* of July 28, 1859.

his post." He wrote many letters to old friends; as if to bid them good-bye.

HIS VIEWS OF LIFE AT FOUR-SCORE.

His state of mind and his views of life at four-score will appear from two of these letters. The first was addressed to the Rev. E. H. Cumpston, of Virginia:

"My Dear Brother,—I thank you for sending me your newspaper article; and the affectionate letter which contained it. . . . . I sent you by mail a pamphlet containing a 'Seminary Address' of mine, and a small volume of 'Discussions in Theology,' which I published about two years ago. The 'Discussions' show with precision the essentials of my religious creed; and the 'Address' gives my view of the great business of the ministry, and the condition of success in it. I feel that in trying to teach others, I, at best, do little more than try to perform the whetstone's office, (*fungar vice cotis;*) 'sharpen without being myself sharp.' Too often, I fear, I have to tremble at the Lord's denunciation of the lawyers, who laid heavy burdens on men's shoulders, which they themselves would not touch with one of their fingers. Pray for me, that I may not be judged out of my own mouth. You say, you have seen of late no mention of my name in the papers. What right has it to be there? What have I done, what have I been, that I should be spoken of in public? Looking at my life, as I am in the habit of doing now, under the instructions of death and the judgment, I feel that, *a parte Dei,* silence in regard to me is infinitely more than my desert! Not a negative treatment, not bare neglect, is the due measure of my recompense from God. Moreover, I have had my day. It is but in the order of nature that I should decrease, while others are increasing. Blessed be God, it might have been worse with me than it has been! Had He left me to myself, what and where would I have been to-day!

"I have not recalled the prayer to which you refer: I desire to depart in *mediis rebus;* with the harness on, as you say.* My health is very good; in my eightieth year, my locomotive faculties are almost as vigorous as they were when I was young. I am punctual at my Seminary labors. Except preaching and writing, I do as much work as I have been accustomed to do. Writing has become more difficult, not from a failure of my intellectual powers, but from an enlarged comprehension of the topics which I treat. In that I am still at my work, and I hope my prayer will be answered. Let me be harnessed for labor! "Affectionately yours,

"T. H. SKINNER."

The other letter was addressed to an old friend and ministerial associate, the Rev. Dr. Helfenstein, of Germantown, Pennsylvania.

"NEW YORK, January 9, 1871,
160 West Twenty-third street.

"REVEREND AND DEAR BROTHER,—A few days since I was informed by the Rev. Dr. Ganse, of this city, that in your retirement from pastoral work you are not in good health; and my regard for you as, for nearly half a

---

* "The prayer referred to, and which he could not recall, was one which our beloved brother Dr. Stiles heard him offer some ten years ago, and which he told me determined him, also, to die with his harness on, and which led him to undertake the arduous work to which his old age is so successfully devoted."—E. H. C.

century, a faithful minister and disciple of our Divine Master and Saviour, and a reminiscence of you as accompanying me to a death-bed scene not far from my dwelling, when I resided on Race street; and also your kindness in sending me a volume of your sermons, incline me, as I cannot 'see you and speak face to face,' 'with ink and pen to write unto you.'

"You and I are very near the end of our course. I am, I think, a little in advance of you—near, very near, the brink of the river; nay, I often say to my friends, I have one foot in the river; and little is left to me but to look about me and cross it! How I should like to be with you and talk with you about our life-experiences, and our prospects as to the eternal future, on which we shall so soon enter! Concerning one thing I am sure we should find ourselves of the same mind, namely, that none among all mankind have been more favored than ourselves as to *the life-work* which was assigned us by the singular grace of God. Could any angel have coveted a greater calling than that in which we have spent our days? Preaching to poor, perishing men the unsearchable riches of Christ! Blessed be God that *this*—not heaping up treasures on earth, not making ourselves a name among scholars, and the worldly wise, and great politicians, and place-seekers—has been our occupation. I am constantly lamenting over my shortcomings, my little profiting by all my advantages and opportunities of serving the Lord, and my countless infirmities and sins; and I sometimes wish, in view of my mistakes and failures, that I could begin my course again; but notwithstanding all my drawbacks, I cannot but call on my soul and all that is within me to bless the Lord that I have been, here on earth, not a banker, or lawyer, or statesman, or prince, but a poor preacher of the everlasting Gospel. And I am sure that in this you are like me; and how should we rejoice together in the wonderful grace of God toward us in this respect, if we could talk with each other of the ministry we have almost completed!

"You, doubtless, know that I was at the funeral of Albert Barnes. Brother, I was never present at such obsequies. I never took part in carrying a man like brother Barnes to his burial. He has not left his equal among us. He is the object of my profound admiration. What a model of industry, of meekness, of patience, of Christian simplicity and dignity was this very extraordinary man! Well, brother, we hope soon to see him again; and also to see brother Patterson, and others whom we have loved and admired as ministers of Christ; and to see Whitefield, and Edwards, and Baxter, and Howe; and to see Paul, and John, and Peter, and all the holy apostles and martyrs; and oh! infinitely more than all, to see, face to face, our blessed and adorable Lord and Saviour Himself!

"Farewell! In the bonds of the everlasting covenant,

"Yours, THOMAS H. SKINNER."

He continued to perform his usual duties in the Seminary until the 24th of January, when he was confined to his house by a severe cold. It was not, however, until Tuesday the 31st, that very serious alarm was felt by his friends; he himself felt no alarm whatever; but on Wednesday forenoon, February 1st, a little before eleven o'clock, the Son of Man came quickly and took him home to Himself.*

It is wonderful to think what astonishment and joy must have been his, on finding himself so suddenly in the presence of his Saviour. Truly, the day of such a man's death is the natal day of eternity. But unspeakable as was the gain to him, how heavy the loss to us! Never again shall we here look upon his benignant, apostolic face, or meet him walking, with quick, nervous step, these earthly streets; never again will he sit where our eyes so delighted to see him sitting, in the chapel, or in the sanctuary, which he loved; no more will he join his voice with ours in singing, "Nearer, my God, to Thee! Nearer to Thee," "Jesus, lover of my soul," "Rock of ages, cleft for me," "My Jesus, as thou wilt." We have felt for the last time that cordial grasp of his hand, which we used to wait for as for a closing benediction; henceforth his Christian brethren and we all shall miss his high, spiritual converse. Precious privileges were these, but they are gone. That dear, benignant face is gazing in rapture upon the Beatific Vision; he who but yesterday was sitting here with us, is seated now with the risen Son of God, in His throne; that voice is joining in the eternal new song; that loving hand has touched adoringly the Hand once nailed, for his and our salvation, to the bitter cross; our old friend has

---

* A few details respecting his last hours, as also some account of the funeral, will be found in Appendix A.

walked and will walk for aye the golden streets of the city of Immanuel.

> "Oh what sweet company
> He there doth hear and see!
> What harmony doth there abound!
> While souls unnumbered sing
> The praise of Zion's King,
> Nor one dissenting voice is found!"

Thanks be to God, who early called him to be a saint, crowned his long life with such sacred beauty, enabled him to bring forth so much fruit, and then gave him the victory, through our Lord Jesus Christ.

How fast the aged ministers, who were his contemporaries and fellow-laborers in the Gospel, are passing away! Only one here and there is any longer to be seen among us. The great majority are at rest in God. And the few, that remain, must often feel like exclaiming:

> "They are all gone into the world of light,
> And I alone sit lingering here!"

But for his aged brethren, who still survive, and for us all, a precious solace is left:

> "Their very memory is fair and bright,
> And my sad thoughts doth clear.
>
> "It glows and glitters in my cloudy breast,
> Like stars upon some gloomy grove,
> Or those faint beams in which the hill is drest,
> After the sun's remove.
>
> I see them walking in an air of glory,
> Whose light doth trample on my days;
> My days, which are at best both dull and hoary,
> Mere glimmering and decays.

> O holy hope! and high humility!
> High as the heavens above!
> These are your walks, and ye have show'd them me,
> To kindle my cold love."

He has gone to be with his Lord; but we have not lost him. There is no parting friends in Christ. He is nearer than ever now. "Heaven is not long to wait, nor far to go." Saints on earth and saints in glory, if not on one floor, are yet under one roof and form one family. Death has taken our venerated friend and brother from our sight, but not from our hearts. We never loved him as we love him now; never was his power over us greater; never his image so fair and Christ-like. His immense faith will still quicken ours; his godly virtues will still impregnate the air we breathe; the prayers he used to offer are yet potent for our advantage; we shall often be thinking of him, and whenever we think of him, it will be a new stimulus to holy living; earth will always be pleasanter because he has been here, and heaven more real and attractive because he has gone there. Wherefore, we praise and bless thee, O God, for his most useful life, for his good example, for his precious love and fellowship; we praise and bless Thee, also, that in a ripe old age, with faculties unbroken, standing firmly at his post, radiant in spiritual beauty, full of the Holy Ghost and of faith, Thou hast taken him home to Thyself. Prepare us, we beseech Thee, when our appointed hour shall strike, to follow him into the unseen world, and there have our rest and portion with him in the life everlasting!

Now unto Him that is able to do exceeding abundantly above all that we ask or think, according to the power that worketh in us, unto Him be glory in the church by Christ Jesus, throughout all ages, world without end. Amen.

APPENDIX.

APPENDIX.

A, PAGE 90.

THE funeral of Dr. Skinner took place on Saturday, February 4th, at the Church of the Covenant. It was a most impressive scene, and will never be forgotten by those who witnessed it. The services in the church were conducted by the Rev. Dr. Prentiss, the Pastor; Prof. Henry B. Smith, of the Union Theological Seminary, and Rev. William Adams, D. D., Pastor of the Madison square Presbyterian church; the singing was by a choir of students. After reading a portion of the 17th chapter of the Gospel of John, Dr. Prentiss gave a sketch of the life and character of the deceased, with some account of his last hours. The following passages are taken from this address :

"Whether regarded as a preacher of the gospel, as a theologian, or as a disciple of Jesus, he was alike admirable and pre-eminent. For almost three-score years he has been identified with the religious interests of the country — especially with the history and piety of the Presbyterian Church. His name has long been a household word among Christian people all over the land; and henceforth it will be embalmed with those of Miller and Richards and Alexander and Beecher and Albert Barnes, and others like them. He came upon the stage at a moment when the theological and ecclesiastical atmosphere foreboded strife and trouble; and, when the storm burst, nobody took a manlier part, nobody was more faithful to his honest convictions, avowed them with greater boldness, or maintained them with more ability, than he. But I shall not dwell upon these things now. Dr. Skinner regarded it as a special favor of Providence, and one of his greatest felicities on earth, that he was permitted, during the closing hours of life, to breathe an atmosphere no longer embittered either by theological or ecclesiastical animosity and discord. One of the last things I saw him do was to grasp the hand of a friend, and exclaim: 'Yes, brother, I believe with you, that the *odium theologicum* is dying out!' From the first, he earnestly desired and prayed for the Reunion of the Presbyterian Church, both for its own sake, and as the harbinger of a larger and still more blessed union of all Christ's disciples; and when the momentous act was at length consummated, his joy was unbounded. Some present will remember how he poured out that joy in this very place, as at the request of the Moderator, although himself not a member of the General Assembly, he offered up thanks to Almighty God immediately after the unanimous vote in favor of Reunion. His whole soul was filled with the spirit of our Lord's high-priestly prayer, that His followers might all be one; *as Thou, Father, art in me, and I in Thee, that they also may be one in us; that the world may believe that Thou hast sent me.* The 17th chapter of the Gospel of John seemed, indeed, to have become part of his spiritual lifeblood. To hear him talk and pray about union with Christ, and the union of Christ's people in Him, was almost like reading, on one's knees, that wonderful chapter.

"Of Dr. Skinner's career and character as preacher and theologian, my brethren, who follow me, will speak. In the earlier and palmy days of his ministry, his power in the pulpit must have been extraordinary. He was little more than a stripling when he began to declare the way of salvation; but even then some of the greatest preachers and divines of the age listened to him with delight, and bore witness to his remarkable gifts. It is related, that on one occasion, he was to preach at Germantown; and, upon entering the pulpit, saw among his hearers, that prince of sacred orators, the renowned Dr. John M. Mason, who happened to be sojourning in the place. At first, he was filled with dismay; but by a special effort of mind, threw himself upon the help of his Master, and was enabled to proceed in his discourse with entire freedom. When the service was over, Dr. Mason came forward, seized him by the hand, and with tears in his eyes, said: 'God bless you! And He *will* bless you!' The latter half of his course in Philadelphia, in the Arch street church, Dr. Skinner called "the seed-time of his ministry;" but every part of his ministry, in Philadelphia, in New England, and in New York, was a seed-time, out of which most precious harvests of souls have been gathered.

"Of his personal and Christian character it is difficult to speak in measured terms. He was a man of the rarest courtesy, grace and sweetness of manners. He had a most winning smile, and when in his high and radiant moods, the charm of his presence and conversation was something indescribable. At such times his face was as it had been the face of an angel. Only two weeks ago to-night, a large number of his brethren saw him in such a mood at his own house; and never will the hallowed scene, or the sweet hymn, 'My Jesus, as Thou wilt,' which he repeated to them at its close, be effaced from their memory.*

* "Now that he is taken, we can see how he has been long preparing for the change. Often as we walked home together from our Saturday night meetings, we have asked how it seemed to be approaching the end of life, and found that his mind was in perfect peace. Only a few days before his death, the Chi Alpha, an association of the ministers of this city, which he greatly loved, met at his house. At the close, as we were about to unite in prayer, he wished that we might join him in singing a particular hymn, and as he could not lay his hand upon the book, he repeated the three

"I never knew a human being of whom it could be said with more truth : *Behold an Israelite indeed, in whom there is no guile !* His artless simplicity was as uncommon as the vigor of his intellect, the beauty of his affections and the sanctity of his life. What he said of his venerated and faithful friend, Dr. James P. Wilson, applied, word for word, to himself: 'What a charm is there in gifts, when simplicity exercises them; and how venerable is simplicity when it invests illustrious gifts! Never have we seen the person in whom simplicity dwelt in a higher degree. Whether in his public ministrations, or in private life, this eminent man was unassuming as a little child, claiming no distinctions above the plainest indi-

verses. We see him now, standing before the fire-place, with his back to the fire, with his hands crossed, and repeating fervently these words :

"'My Jesus, as Thou wilt!
O may Thy will be mine ;
Into Thy hand of love,
I would my all resign ;
Through sorrow or through joy,
Conduct me as Thine own,
And help me still to say,
My Lord, Thy will be done.

"'My Jesus, as Thou wilt!
Though seen through many a tear,
Let not my star of hope
Grow dim, or disappear ;
Since Thou on earth hast wept,
And sorrowed oft alone,
If I must weep with Thee,
My Lord, Thy will be done !

"'My Jesus, as thou wilt !
All shall be well for me ;
Each changing future scene,
I gladly trust with Thee ;
Straight to my home above
I travel calmly on,
And sing, in life, or death,
My Lord, Thy will be done !'"

—*The Evangelist*, February 9th.

vidual, and appearing to be conscious of no superiority to him in any kind of excellence.' To this lovely trait was joined a humility equally remarkable. One of the church fathers, on being asked what is the first thing in religion, replied, Humility—and what the second, replied, Humility—and what the third, replied still, Humility. It was so in an eminent degree with our departed friend. He loved to lie low—'*infinitely* low,' as his favorite, President Edwards, expresses it, before God. He was very modest and humble in reference to his intellectual and theological gifts and attainments; while the sense of his own unworthiness, littleness, and imperfections as a minister and disciple of Jesus, was overpowering, and would have been intolerable, had it not been relieved and swallowed up by impassioned love to his Saviour, and an immense faith in Him. The depth and intensity of both sentiments were strikingly illustrated by an incident, which occurred only a few days before his last illness. He called at my house for the purpose of spiritual conference with a Christian friend. Before leaving, he said: 'I have brought something which I want to read to you,' intimating that it expressed exactly his own feeling. He then read, with infinite animation and emphasis, and with holy unction beaming in his eye and face, a letter of Rev. William Romaine, author " Life, Walk and Triumph of Faith." The letter is so striking, and throws such light upon the state of his own soul, that I give a large portion of it:

"'Blessed be the God and Father of our Lord Jesus Christ, who hath blessed you with so many blessings already, and who, having begun, will not cease to bless you in life and death, and forever more! Your letter of May 2d puts me in mind of His goodness, as I wish all things may. It rejoices my very heart to see Him displaying the glories of His grace far and wide. From London through Europe, from Europe to America, yea, as far as the sun travels, His fame is spread. And does He not deserve it? Oh, my friend, what have we to tell of but the loving-kindness of Jesus; and what to praise but His wonders in saving such as we are, and in saving so many of us? Blessings forever on the Lamb! May we glorify Him by resting on Him for righteousness and strength, and by living wholly upon Him for grace and glory. Then all goes well, when

> "'On all besides his precious blood,
> On all besides the Son of God,
> We trample boldly, and disclaim
> All other saviours but the *Lamb*.

"'As to what you write about, I know not what to say. It is in the best hands. He knows what to do. Let Him alone. Remember He is the head of the Church, and He will look after His own matters, and well, too. At present, I see not my way clearly from London. Here my Master fixes me, and here I must stay till He calls me to some other place. When He would have me to move, He will let me know His will. Besides, what am I? What does it signify where I am? A poor, dumb dog, the vilest, the basest of all the servants of my Lord. If you could see what is passing for any one hour in my heart, you would not think anything of me; you would only admire and extol the riches of Jesus' love. Wonderful it is that He should send such an one to preach His gospel, and bless it, to many, many souls (while every sermon covers me with shame and confusion)—oh, this is wonderful, wonderful, eternally to be admired, grace! What cannot He do? who can form a preacher out of such a dry, rotten stick, fit for nothing but the fire of hell? Glory, glory be to Him alone, and forever and forever more. All the tongues in heaven and in earth, men and angels, throughout eternity, cannot praise Him enough for what He has already done for my soul, and, therefore, I am content to be a poor, broken, bankrupt debtor forever. Hereby I shall be enabled forever to exalt Him, and to put the crown upon His head, and that is all I want. It will be heaven enough to join that blessed company, who are crying, *Worthy is the Lamb* (but none else) *to receive power and riches and wisdom and strength and honor and glory and blessing.*'"

"Of many other things—of his devotional habits and his marvelous gift in prayer—of his noble virtues as a Christian citizen and patriot—of his relations to his old church in Mercer street, to this bereaved church of the Covenant, and to myself as his pastor in both, I would gladly speak; but time forbids' that I should do so now. I hasten to the closing hours.

"The death of his old and greatly beloved friend, Mr. Barnes, made a profound impression upon him; and after his return from Philadelphia, I felt that he might slip away from us at any moment. His heart and his thoughts were, plainly, all above, where Christ sitteth at the right hand of God. In a letter to an old friend in Boston, dated January 24th, only a week before his departure, he writes: 'What a glorious death was that of Albert Barnes! It holds me wondering and praising God for His singular grace to that very remarkable man. Is it possible that such a death is to be mine? I wish to die, if God's will be so, in *mediis rebus;* but to die in *good health* and *without pain!* Is such a mercy in reserve for me? Pray for me, my dear friend, that die, when, where, or how I may, I may glorify God in dying.'

"But, although suffering from a cold, he continued his lectures, as usual, until Wednesday of last week. On Thursday, a physician was called in; but it was not until Tuesday morning of this week, that his friends became very seriously alarmed at his condition.* His prostration was at that time exceedingly great. He lay dozing

---

* On Monday evening, as the night wore on, he said to the members of his family about him: "You can leave me now and I will compose myself to sleep." One of them, however, unobserved by him, remained in the darkened room. He immediately, with the simplicity of a child, repeated to himself a portion of Scripture, recited the whole of his favorite hymn, "My Jesus, as Thou wilt," and then offered aloud his evening prayer.

at intervals throughout the day, rarely speaking, save in reply to questions, and evidently disinclined to mental exertion of any sort. Towards evening he was much agitated and disturbed by an effort to take nourishment. An attempt was therefore made to divert his mind from painful thoughts by speaking of Christ. He instantly caught at the allusion, and though he had hitherto spoken little, and that with great difficulty, his whole soul roused itself, and he broke forth into the most wonderful expressions of love to his Saviour, closing with the following stanzas from a hymn of Watts, which he repeated with such unction and energy of feeling, that, at the time, the language was not recognized as verse, but was supposed to be his own. That it was the language of his inmost heart at that very moment, no one who had heard the tones, and seen the worn, yet illumined face, could for an instant doubt:

> "' Lord, when I quit this earthly stage,
> Where shall I fly, but to Thy breast?
> For I have sought no other home:
> For I have learned no other rest.
>
> "' I cannot live contented here
> Without some glimpses of Thy face;
> And heaven, without Thy presence there,
> Will be a dark and tiresome place.
>
> "' When earthly cares engross the day,
> And hold my thoughts aside from Thee,
> The shining hours of cheerful light
> Are long and tedious years to me.
>
> "' And if no evening visit's paid
> Between my Saviour and my soul,
> How dull the night! how sad the shade!
> How mournfully the minutes roll!
>
> "' This flesh of mine might learn as soon
> To live, yet part with all my blood;
> To breathe, when vital air is gone,
> Or thrive and grow without my food.

> "'The strings that twine about my heart,
>   Tortures and racks may tear them off;
> But they can never, never part
>   With their dear hold of Christ, my Love.
>
> "'My God! and can an humble child,
>   Who loves Thee with a flame so high,
> Be ever from Thy face exiled,
>   Without the pity of Thine eye?
>
> "'Impossible! For Thine own hands
>   Have tied my heart so fast to Thee;
> And in Thy book the promise stands,
>   That where Thou art, Thy friends must be.'

"His physicians saw him early on Wednesday morning, and thought he might perhaps live through the day. But he sank rapidly, and his mind was more or less bewildered through his physical exhaustion. There was now and then a whispered word, 'more faith,' 'blessed Saviour,' 'a poor sinner,' but most of what he said was unintelligible. At about a quarter before eleven, he said, with almost a smile: 'I feel a *great deal better*, and am going to get up.' Yielding to the solicitation to remain in bed, he lay quietly for a moment, then rose and sat upright for a single instant. A sudden pallor spread over his face, and he was tenderly replaced upon his pillow, where he drew his breath gently at intervals, but so gently that those who watched about him hardly knew at what moment the ardent soul took flight from the exhausted body."

Professor Smith then spoke as follows:

"Our revered father and brother in the Christian ministry was connected with the Union Theological Seminary of this city, as a Director from its beginning in 1836, and as its Professor of Sacred Rhetoric, Pastoral Theology, and Church Government for nearly a quarter of a century. Of those who were with him in its foundation, only three survive—Dr. Adams, Mr. Charles Butler, (now President of the Board of Directors,) and Mr. Fisher Howe, of Brooklyn. Our Seminary owes as much to Dr. Skinner as to any other man; in some respects, especially in its spiritual power and history, it owes more to him than to any other man. I am to say a few words on what he was to us, and of our special loss. This is not the time to speak of him in the details of his life's work.

"A theological seminary needs to be poised upon a spiritual centre; not only to be rooted in Christ the Head, but also to centre in some visible impersonation of the spiritual power of a living Christian faith, animating its members by example and by word. That was the position which our venerable senior Professor held (all unconsciously to himself) to both the Faculty and the students of this Institution. Such spiritual force is silent, it is not much spoken of; but its loss is felt as we feel the setting of the sun. It comes—it can come—only from a life instinct with the powers of the world to come; it cannot be born of the will of man; it cannot be bought—the price of it is above rubies; it is fashioned by divine grace, and its presence is felt rather than defined.

"Dr. Skinner came to us in the full vigor of his intellect, and gave to our students the wisest and maturest labors of his lengthened life. The brilliant enthusiasm of his earliest ministry in Philadelphia, heightened by its conflicts; the ardent and pungent evangelism, the flaming logic, of his memorable service in the Mercer street church, built by and for him; his varied and earnest studies; his catholic spirit, and his settled Presbyterian convictions—all worked in and enabled him, at an age when most men think of retiring from their labors, to achieve high repute in a new work. He was nearly three-score years of age when he began his instructions to our classes: but very few men have such tenacity and elasticity of both body and mind. One reason of his endurance and success is, that he wisely stuck to his proper work.

"His old age, the period commonly so called, was indeed remarkable. Few men whose lives are so long spared are what he was. He never outlived his enthusiasm for anything good and true, even though it might be new. On the themes that interested him he would light up to the last with the fervor of youth. In his higher mental powers he did not seem to grow old. Now and then the brightness of his eye was dimmed, his hearing became a shade less acute, his abstraction from external things was somewhat more noticeable; but his intellect remained clear and intent; his soul grew larger with his growing years, and the scope of his spiritual vision was widened as he mounted higher and higher. How easily he surpassed us all in spiritual discernment.

"And this was what distinguished him: while living in the world he lived above the world. I have never known a more unwordly character. He was absorbed by a higher life. The so-called fascinations and distractions of this teeming metropolis were no temptations to him; he was among them but not of them; they just glanced off from his untarnished shield. And even in the Church he could never understand manœuvring and ecclesiastical politics; he knew so little about such by-means that he was really amazed at them. He just thought and said what seemed true, and did what seemed right, and all the rest was no concern of his, somebody would take care of it. And he was so single-minded that, had the necessity come, he would, I doubt not, have marched to the stake singing the song of victory. He believed in another life.

"In Plato's immortal description of the cave and the light, he tells us that the dwellers in the cave when they come to the light seem to others to be dazed. There is always a kind of abstraction about great thinkers, poets, and divines. Common people cannot quite see through them. They speak from a larger view and to a greater audience than that of their own generation. Mutely they appeal to a coming tribunal. And so our departed friend was at times engrossed and absorbed in the high subjects of Christian thought. He pondered them by day and by night. He saw them from the Mount of Vision. He described them in glowing periods. His fellowship was with the Father and the Son. If he thought and spake less of the things of time, it was because like Paul he was rapt in a higher sphere—where God's 'glory smote him in the face.'

"He was to the last a reader, a student, and a thinker. No student in the Seminary had a keener relish for hard work than he, or found more to learn. Until within two or three years he was always re-writing his lectures and even his sermons. His most carefully prepared work, his 'Discussions in Theology,' an admirable book, was published only three years ago. Some of the essays in it are not only complete in their anatomy, but are finished with the refined art of a sculptor.

"And the same volume also defines his theological position. In seeking for truth he never seemed to ask, what is the view of my side, but what is the truth itself? He did not take his definitions from any man. Cordially attached to the theology of the Reformed churches, he was always willing to merge lesser differences for the sake of the unity and prosperity of the Church.

"His seminary duties were not official tasks; he loved his work, and it grew upon him. His lectures on Church Government, and Sacred Rhetoric, and the Pastoral Office, were wrought out with comprehensive thought and care. To the very last he read all new works on these subjects, though he did not find in them much that was new to him. But he praised many a book, and many a sermon, rather from the fulness of his own vision than from what others could find in them.

"All true human greatness is also humble; it does not seem to seek its own. With his acknowledged superiority, how deferential was our brother to others, even to men of low estate! It was sometimes embarrassing to us to find that he was not aware of his own superior position. He was among us as one that serveth. There was about him a certain grace of manner, an old-time chivalry of tone (now almost a tradition) towards those less and younger and weaker than himself, which showed the true nobility of his soul. It came from his high sense of personal honor, which made him honor all men. He was magnanimous, because he was humble.

"And what a helper and friend he was! His personal affections were unswerving. When I came here, he took me by the hand, and its cordial pressure was never relaxed. When the pastor of this church succeeded him in the ministry, no one greeted him, and no one has clung to him, as did he. He was never weary of talking of his old friends at home in North Carolina, of Dr. Wilson, and brother Patterson, and Albert Barnes—with whom he was united in life, and by death not long divided,—of his teachers and class-mates in Nassau Hall. What he was as a husband and a father—dearest of all earthly names—they only fully know who to-day mourn most deeply and are most deeply comforted.

"A thousand of his pupils, all over our country and in many a distant land, mourn with us his loss; and many thousands to whom he preached the Gospel, will sorrow for him who led them to Christ, and by his own life showed the way

"As a teacher in the Presbyterian Church he was cordially attached to its doctrine and government. But this did not exclude, it rather favored, his love for the whole body of Christ. It not only gave him zeal for our auspicious reunion, but enlarged his love for all who profess and call themselves Christians. His charity could not be bounded by the confines of any sect. He believed more fully in the invisible than in the visible Church. He loved all the brethren, and labored for all men.

"His power and influence as a theological teacher were also increased by his keen sense of the honor and dignity of his own profession. In this he was not humble, for he spake from a high calling. Necessity was laid upon him. No student could doubt that he really felt, Woe is unto me and to you, if we do not preach the Gospel, for eternity is here at stake. No one could doubt that he truly believed the ministry of the Gospel to be the highest and the most serviceable office which man can fill, that of an ambassador for Christ, at the service of all men for their spiritual welfare.

" His personal power was also enhanced, year by year, with the increase of his spiritual life; while the outward man was perishing, the inward man was renewed day by day. He became more and more a living Epistle, a Gospel of God's grace, known and read of all men. Vexed and perplexing questions were merged in a higher life. Revealed facts took the place of disputed propositions. The living Christ took the place of the doctors of the schools, and with advantage.

" Thus he lived and grew day by day, in his serene and hallowed old age, towards the measure of the stature of a perfect man in Christ Jesus. Was he, then, a saint on earth? He was *called* to be a saint, and he was always fulfilling his calling, not counting himself to have attained, but ever pressing onward. Upon the whole I think he was as saint-like a man as any of us have ever seen.

" So he lived on, with his wiry and flexible frame, mind and body active to the last. Every succeeding winter we have thought might be too much for him. But he bore up bravely—till he touched the verge of four-score years. The shadows of his life lengthened, but he saw not the shadows, for his face was turned to the light. Ten days ago I met him at the Seminary for the last time; and his grasp was as firm and his look as warm as ever; though even then he said: " I cannot long be with you." He went out into the piercing cold—its rigor seized upon him, its fatal grasp could not be loosened; his time had come; his Master called, and he was always ready. Of death he had no fear, though he sometimes said that he shrank from dying. But at last even this natural fear passed away, and he could say with a full heart:

> "Welcome the hour of full discharge,
> Which sets my longing soul at large,
> Unbinds my chains, breaks up my cell,
> And gives me with my God to dwell."

"To him 'dying was but going home.' Peacefully he passed away as a child to its rest. He has gone where there is no more Winter: there everlasting Spring abides. He is with the patriarchs and apostles and saints and brethren he loved so well; and yet he hardly sees them in his impassioned vision of One whose name is above every name, and whose image was upon his soul. He has heard the welcome, 'Well done, good and faithful servant, enter thou into the joy of thy Lord.' And over his grave we can only say—mastering our grief—Blessed are the dead who die in the Lord."

The following is the substance of Dr. Adams's remarks:

"The world will seem much more lonely to very many, because this eminent servant of God has gone out of it; but how much better for the world, because he has lived in it!

"To utter his eulogy is to be rebuked by the remembrance of his modesty. Why did he hold so high a place in the esteem of all? Because he was so lowly in his own. Why were all disposed to defer to him and to honor him? Because he never obtruded himself upon any. So exquisite was his taste, so highly cultivated his religious sensibility, that he was accustomed to shrink from any reference to himself. While, at proper times, in proper places, for high uses he displayed the thoroughness of his self-knowledge, the profound skill and honesty of his self-analysis, he did not abound in profuse allusions to his own spiritual experience, for that was too deep and sacred to be evaporated in flippant speech. There is a lesson in this which is good for all. One should never make a turnpike of his heart for promiscuous travel. There is an exposure of one's own mind scarcely less indecorous than that of the person. The memory of what Dr. Skinner truly was, makes one to weigh every word concerning him with a most cautious regard to his refined, sensitive, and delicate sense of propriety.

"His career as a Christian preacher began in times of sharp theological controversy. His mind was too eager and active, and his logical habits of thought were too exact to allow him to be indifferent to the questions then in debate; but never did he suffer himself to be diverted from his one great work as a preacher of the 'glorious Gospel of the blessed God.' His nicest metaphysical distinctions all came into play, not as arid learning, but as practical helps, when in the pulpit he commended the truth to the human conscience in the sight of God.

"The period, in which the best part of his ministerial life was spent, was distinguished by those extraordinary effusions of the Holy Spirit, which were hardly less remarkable than 'the great awakening' in the last century, as associated with the pen and preaching of Jonathan Edwards. With the quickest instinct he interpreted, and with the warmest sympathy he entered into that great work of God. It gave a peculiar point and character to all his preaching through life. So thorough was his self-conviction as to the truth, that he seemed always to expect that others would be convinced also. He unfolded and enforced the truth as with the utmost confidence of success. He cherished an attachment for his profession which amounted to a noble and fervent enthusiasm. Like George Herbert, whom, in many points he resembled, he regarded his pulpit as his 'joy and throne.' So earnest was his manner, and glowing his discourse, that he always made the impression on his hearers that he expected, and with good reason, an immediate verdict, and was disappointed if it was not given. Those memorable scenes in

Philadelphia, in New Haven, in New York, when preaching with such demonstrations of the Spirit and of power, inquirers and converts were computed by hundreds and thousands, and a whole audience bent toward him like a field of grain! Then was it that he plied his sickle well, and filled his bosom with many sheaves. How many are already garnered in the kingdom of heaven, how many still living in these churches and pulpits, who will always hail him as the chosen means of mercy to their souls!

"Dr. Skinner was, to use an expression, which in old English bore a peculiar sense, a perfect Christian GENTLEMAN. He was a specimen of spiritual beauty. How pure, how gentle, how guileless, how kind, how courteous, how free from all suspicion of worldly ambition! How sweet his latest experience! How often has it been said of him by his friends, 'He is fast ripening for heaven.' Like ripe fruit has he fallen, in its time, detached by no violence. Age had impaired none of his faculties, only imparted additional serenity to his countenance, sweetness to his manners, and beauty to his character, as the disc of the setting sun seems to be larger, and its lustre to be softer than when in its meridian. How calmly has he been sitting in his stall in the cathedral of life, with the banner of Christ's love over his head, waiting for the service to be over, that he might say with all his heart, Amen. That word he has pronounced; and he has received the end of his faith the salvation of his soul.

"How nigh heaven is brought to us by such translations! How fast heaven is enriching itself with the spoils gathered from our friendships, our homes, churches and pulpits!"

At the close of the services in the church, the remains were taken to the Marble Cemetery on Second street. They were borne by the students of Union Theological Seminary, the following clergymen acting as pall-bearers: Rev. Dr. De Witt, Reformed; Rev. Dr. Anderson, Baptist; Bishop Janes, Methodist; Rev. Samuel H. Cox, D.D., Presbyterian; Rev. Dr. Tyng, Episcopal; Rev. Dr. Hutton, Reformed; Rev. Dr. Paxton, Presbyterian; Rev. Dr. Cheever, Congregationalist. The closing benediction, at the grave, was pronounced by the venerable Bishop Janes.

At one o'clock, an hour before the public obsequies, a meeting of clergymen of different denominations, belonging to New York and its vicinity, was held in the chapel of the Church of the Covenant, at which the Rev. Dr. Murray, Pastor of the Brick Church, presided. It was thus referred to in the *Observer* of the following week:

"How beautiful the last scenes in the earthly history of the beloved and honored Dr. Skinner. His brethren in the ministry, of all names, came together, crowding the chapel till no more could enter, and then they spake one to another of his graces and his gifts, how the spirit of the Master shone in his face and words and ways; how pure and simple and childlike he was; how wise, and great and good! And old men told of their debts to him for impressions made on them for life when they were young, and others said the world to come could alone reveal the extent and fullness of his power. And they asked to have the coffin with his remains brought in among them, that they might once more look upon the sweet face they had so long admired and loved. His loving students took him up with tender hands, and brought him in and laid him down in the midst of the sorrowing company. And the old men—Dr. Spring, older by six years than the departed, Dr. Cox and Dr. De Witt, very nearly the same age—came to the side of the coffin and dropped tears of affection there; and then the younger, but not young men, many of them with white locks and bending with years, passed by; and then the strong men and those in early life, came and looked upon the quiet countenance of him whose soul was even then in the joy of his Lord.

"And when all had taken a last look of their father and friend, the young men carried him out to the church, where the great congregation had met for his funeral.

"It is rare, in the life-time of any of us, that such a funeral service is rendered."

At this meeting in the chapel, very interesting addresses were made by Rev. Dr. S. H. Cox, one of Dr. Skinner's oldest and dearest friends; Rev. Dr. Roche, of the Methodist; Rev. Dr. Rogers, of the Reformed; Rev. Dr. J. P. Thompson, of the Congregational, and Rev. Drs. Tyng and John Cotton Smith, of the Episcopal church. The following minute, prepared and presented by Rev. Dr. Thompson, and seconded by Dr. Tyng, was unanimously adopted:

"We, the clergy of New York and vicinity, assembled to render the last offices of respect and affection to the Rev. Thomas H. Skinner, D.D., so widely venerated and beloved as pastor, teacher, counsellor and friend, reminding ourselves of his own devout and adoring sentiment—that 'it is the chief glory of the divine attributes, that they are all in the service of *Love*'—would humbly acknowledge the dispensation of Providence which has removed him from among us, as but another expression of that Love which qualified him for such usefulness in the Church, and continued him so long, with powers undimmed and with graces ever brightening, in his sphere of honorable and beneficent service. Having accomplished the four-score years of life, and almost three-score years of unabated work in the ministry, having gathered the largest fruits of honor, blessedness and reward in his Master's kingdom upon earth, and having outlived the major part of the co-laborers of his youth and prime, there remained nothing to crown his age and fulfill his joy, but that he should 'depart and be with Christ.'

"Above all would we magnify in his death that grace which rendered him in life so conspicuous, in the rare combination of a noble and disciplined intellect consecrated to truth, a childlike simplicity of faith, and a seraphic fervor of devotion.

"For singleness of aim in personal sanctification, testifying with Paul, 'this one thing I do, reaching forth to those things which are before;' for singleness of purpose in his ministry, as determined with Paul, 'not to know anything save Jesus Christ, and him crucified;' for singleness of devotion, that re-produced in his consciousness the experience of Paul, 'for me to live is Christ;' for loftiness of ideal, that set the Christian character above all earthly standards, and the kingdom of God above all earthly good; for guilelessness of spirit, that exemplified the meekness and gentleness of the children of God; for a courtesy and kindliness that beautified the daily intercourse of life, and adorned his public teaching; for an unction of speech and a saintliness of conversation, that were the open testimony of the Father to his communings with God in secret; for a zeal for God, which ofttimes 'had eaten him up,' had not the doing of the will of God been 'meat and drink' to body and soul; for boldness in declaring the truth and contending for the faith; for a breadth of charity that embraced all that love our Lord Jesus Christ, and a sympathetic yearning for souls that caused him to keep vigils for their salvation; for a grandeur of hope, that kept ever before him the millennial glories as palpable realities, and an exaltation of faith, that held him serene and steadfast above all assaults of the adversary upon his own peace or the peace of the Church, and that seemed at times to lift him out of the body, in his rapturous discourse of the government of God and the glories of redemption; for these manifold and illustrious graces of the Spirit, his memory shall be cherished among us, and be transmitted in the schools of the prophets, as a motive to the highest attainments in excellence and usefulness, and especially to that elevated and cultured piety which is the true strength of the Christian ministry.

"Remembering also how in him metaphysical acumen and logical vigor, profound meditation and persistent study, were applied to the deep things of God, without abating the freshness of his faith, the fervor of his devotion, the enthusiasm of his love, in respect to the simplest doctrines of salvation; how the nicest discrimination and the choicest diction of the Christian scholar were brought to the elucidation of Bible truth; we would make grateful record of such an example of consecrated intellect in this speculative and rationalizing age; and would encourage ourselves and the ministry at large to assert the supreme claim of the Gospel upon all the powers of the human soul.

"In sympathy with the whole Church bereaved of such a leader, we would humbly commend the cause of sacred learning, the pastoral office, the training of the ministry, our several departments of labor in the Christian household, and the personal household of our departed brother with which we share the sorrows, the memories, and the hopes of this hour—to the Great Head of the Church, our sympathizing and comforting Redeemer, who 'continueth ever.'"

The Rev. J. A. Roche, D.D., has kindly furnished the substance of his glowing tribute, which was as follows:

"A distinguished writer has remarked of one whose biography he wrote, that so great were the advantages he was conscious of having received from the wise and weighty teacher of his former years, that he asserted, in his later life, he passed no day without experiencing some benefit from the lessons and example of his honored instructor.

"Such are the obligations I acknowledge in speaking of Dr. Skinner. I had often heard of his remarkable ministry in Philadelphia, where, at a subsequent period, I was a pastor. After my removal to New York, I availed myself of the opportunity of attending his lectures on 'Sacred Rhetoric and Pastoral Theology,' in the Union Theological Seminary. I had been in the ministry more than twenty years. I was not without apprehension that theological seminaries are too nearly, as Rowland Hill expresses it, 'Manufactories to turn out preachers.' With John Newton, I said: 'Only God can make the minister.' But when I heard Dr. Skinner on the call and the devotion to the ministry, the sacrifices to be made, the services to be performed, the sufferings to be accepted, the spirit to be cherished, exhibited, maintained; when I heard him assert the authority, declare the themes, and urge the qualifications—the *Divine qualifications* of the preacher of righteousness; when I saw the breadth of the lecturer's culture, and the nearness of his walk with God; when I witnessed the sweetness and urbanity of his temper, the purity and elevation of his character; when I beheld the stores of his knowledge, and felt the force of his logic, and the power of an elocution that did even transcend his clear, pure, vigorous style; when in his discourse he so 'projected himself,' that the man appeared in the full play and direction of all the faculties and forces of his intellectual and moral being—in the intense earnestness that uniformly distinguished his efforts—when there was felt the influence of his matchless manner, as he urged those before him, not only to preach Christ, but to preach Christ crucified, not simply Christ as an example, but in His death as an atonement; when I saw from week to week, from month to month, how he humbled man and exalted God, and what an unction rested on him in his lectures; I was so impressed with the advantages that the young men had in such training, that I went from the seminary, time after time, saying: 'Happy are thy men—happy are these—which stand continually before thee, and that hear thy wisdom.' The language of Rowland Hill dropped from my thoughts when I heard

Dr. Skinner. Not the 'manufactory to turn out preachers,' but the 'school of the prophets,' became my idea of the Theological Seminary.

"For years I have deemed it one of the greatest privileges and richest blessings of my life, that I was permitted to hear and see and feel so much of the instruction and example and spirit of this great and good man, from whom death has now separated us.

"Such was my delight in his lectures, that I twice took the same course. They were to me, at once, an intellectual feast and a means of grace. I am very culpable, if I am not a better thinker, purer Christian, and a more successful preacher, for having so well known Dr. Skinner. Nay, there is cause for self-condemnation, if to-day I am not a better specimen of a man from having enjoyed such intercourse with this one of Nature's noblemen, this one of the 'princes of God's people.'

"To say that I admired him, loved him, is to say too little. How near he was to my ideal man, minister, Christian!

"I never knew so well, how great a sermon can be as a composition, or as a moral power, till I heard him tell it. Truth never seemed like such a projectile as when I saw him launch it. God's ministers never seemed so exalted and the themes of the pulpit so sublime, as when he described the one and declared the other.

"He regarded Jonathan Edwards as equally distinguished as a metaphysician and preacher, and he delighted to show the great power of Edwards in such sermons as 'Sinners in the hands of an angry God,' and when on one occasion, a member of the class asked if 'Such preaching would do in the present day.' He replied, with great animation, 'I would walk fifty miles to hear that sermon.' Twice Dr. S. preached for me in my pulpit, once on 'The Necessity of the New Birth,' once on 'Past Feeling.' The latter sermon I importuned him to publish.

"There was in the movement of his mind, the magnitude of his matter, the weight of his sentences, the force of his arguments, the depth of his feeling, and the afflatus that rested upon him, that which made him seem majestic. He awed me. A distinguished physician and professor of medical science in Philadelphia, once told me, 'He never saw God till Dr. Skinner showed Him.' Then he 'abhorred himself.' I have known no ministry, that in my estimate, more nearly assimilated to Edwards than that of Skinner.

"He was a Presbyterian, I a Methodist; but as he stated the doctrines he believed and taught, there was in me no heart for controversy. It is an humble tribute that I can pay to so good and great a man, but I can show my heart.

"In my preparations for the pulpit, in my labors of the pastorate, in my cheerful acceptance of the privations of the sacred calling, in my enthusiasm for the work, and in my superiority of mind and heart to all the discouragements of the gospel ministry, I pass no day without some advantage derived from this master in Israel, whose memory I so cherish. How much earth loses when such a man is taken. How much heaven gains when such a saint enters its portals. It is my joy to anticipate a meeting, when with a greater warmth than ever, I will grasp his hand, and tell him, if I can, how much good he did in helping me to honor that Christ at whose feet he 'casts his crown.'"

The following letter of Rev. Charles Hodge, D.D., addressed to the Faculty of the Union Theological Seminary, will be here in place:

"PRINCETON, *February* 15, 1871.

"DEAR BRETHREN,—When your beloved and revered colleague, Dr. Thomas H. Skinner, was called away, I was ill in bed. I was not informed of his death for more than a week after its occurrence. I wish these facts to be known; because few persons were under stronger obligations to stand at the grave of Thomas H. Skinner than myself; and few had a better right to appear there as a mourner.

"For more than fifty-five years I knew, loved and honored him, and was loved and trusted by him. Of this he often assured me, and no man ever doubted his sincerity.

"You must excuse the personal character of this communication. I cannot forbear entering my claim to be counted among the oldest and most devoted of his friends.

"He was a man by himself. The union of high gifts, with the most transparent, child-like simplicity of character, gave him a peculiar position in the love and admiration of his friends.

"With great respect, yours in Christian bonds,

"CHARLES HODGE."

The following is an extract from Dr. Thayer's sermon, referred to in the discourse:

"*Henceforth there is laid up for me a crown of righteousness, which the Lord, the righteous Judge, shall give me at that day, and not to me only, but unto all them also that love His appearing.* Yes, that was the end of Paul's conflicts on earth. In a moment's time he would be with that beloved and glorious Lord; and when Christ should appear, Paul should also appear with Him in glory. Nor is this true of Paul only. We thank God it is just as true of all who fight the good fight and keep the faith. So, to-day, we think of one more noble spirit who, after a long life of loving service, has entered into the joy of his Lord. We sorrow that we shall see his face no more in this church he loved to frequent, nor hear his voice in the prayer-meeting, from which he was so rarely absent.

Hardly among his own people in New York will Christians mourn for him more than will those of this church, who have enjoyed the benefit of his example, and to whom his words of instruction and his prayers were at times almost inexpressibly quickening and elevating.

"I can hardly trust myself to speak of Dr. Skinner, so highly do I revere his piety, and so much shall I miss his sympathy and help in the work here. But in this world of varnish and shams, and where the imperfections of even good men make anything like eulogy dangerous, it is delightful to speak out fearlessly one's joy in a Christian character universally esteemed. Elsewhere they will dwell upon the different passages of his life, his early conversion when at the South he gave up riches and brilliant prospects in the law for Christ and His ministry. Two pastorates in Philadelphia and New York will afford ample material for observations. His work as teacher of Sacred Rhetoric, will invite attention, while his preaching in the days of his power, and his writings, will be interesting themes. To most of those who knew him here, he appeared chiefly as a vigorous and chastened old age presented him. Seemingly unbroken in powers of mind—as close a student as ever—keeping up fully with modern thought in philosophy and theology and interpretation and sacred rhetoric, he appeared as discriminating as ever. But there was evident in him a wider range—an increasing appreciation of thinkers aside from his own school, and a greater disposition to qualify the statements of opinion. He looked out on society and its relations to Christianity more and more with the large-mindedness of a Christian philosopher. With his memory stored, with his intellectual appetite unabated, with unfeigned pleasure in intelligent discussion, he was a most interesting companion. Pleasant as it is, and not unprofitable, to recall this in one whom I wish to honor before my people, his Christian character was his chief attraction. The fire of his early years was tempered—a certain hardness in his manner, which was rendered more noticeable by the peculiar absence of fancy, and even the emotional, in a restricted sense—was softened down. He was scrupulously free from guile. No man ever suspected him of ulterior design. He was distinguished in his palmy days for plans in his sermons; but aside from them, he followed principles and not plans. It was not the least of his merits that he was too transparent to outwit anybody, and so he never was accused of trying. In lesser things he was not persistent; but in matters of right, Dr. Skinner was the stuff of which real martyrs are made. He proved his superiority to considerations of money too unmistakably to need comment. But after all, we love most to think of his inmost life. His conception of Christianity had no morbid taint in it. To him the law of God was marvelously clear, and awful in its extent and purity, lovely in its moral excellence. So, while full of hope, few men were so sensible of their sins. His views of God were comprehensive and vivid. Hence, it is not often now that you hear such exhibitions of the Divine government. But the soul of his piety was his child-like, clinging faith in Christ; it is in this that he showed most the work of God in his soul. As might be expected, his controlling desire was to please Christ. Can we ever forget his prayers for the Spirit of God? He lived in daily expectation of heaven. He often spoke of it. And now he is there, with the great and good of Christ; and oh, with Christ Himself! I know this is strong language, but I have weighed my words. Do you, my church, estimate the privilege of having had this man of God among you? It is a great loss for us; but oh, it is so great a mercy that he is taken before any weakness came over him— taken in a beautiful old age—as when the sun sets in golden light. Then, to-day, we lift the conqueror's strain for him. 'He has fought a good fight; he has finished his course; he has kept the faith.' 'Henceforth he hath a crown of righteousness, which the Lord, the righteous

Judge, has given him.' Oh, let me die the death of the righteous, and let my last end be like his!"

Immediately upon the death of Dr. Skinner, the Board of Directors and Faculty of the Union Theological Seminary were called together, and appropriate arrangements made for the funeral. Mr. Charles Butler, the President of the Board, and one of the oldest friends of the deceased in New York, offered some very touching remarks; and he was followed by others in the same strain. After the funeral an adjourned meeting took place, when the subjoined Minute, expressive of the sentiment of the Board, was adopted:

"It becomes the painful duty of the Board, for the third time within a year, to record the ravages of death among their beloved co-laborers in the conduct of this Seminary. On two other occasions only, since the founding of the Institution, has a member of the Faculty been removed by death.

"To the honored names of WHITE and ROBINSON, the no less honored name of SKINNER must now be added—patriarchal names, to be had in grateful remembrance, in all coming time, by the friends of Union Seminary.

"The Rev. THOMAS HARVEY SKINNER, D. D., LL. D., the first and only occupant of the Davenport chair of Sacred Rhetoric, Pastoral Theology and Church Government, departed this life, in the full enjoyment of a blissful hope of immortality, on Wednesday, February 1, 1871, having almost completed the eightieth year of his age, and the fifty-eighth year of his continuous active service in the ministry of the gospel—full of honors as of years.

"Our departed friend and brother had been identified with the history and interests of this school of the prophets, from its very foundation. Called in the year 1835 from the Professorship of Sacred Rhetoric, in Andover

Theological Seminary, to be the first pastor of the Mercer street Presbyterian church of this city, he entered with characteristic ardor into the project of creating a similar institution, to be located in the great metropolis, on the largest scale of usefulness, as called for by the demands of the Church, in her vastly extending operations, and the wants of the age.

"Chosen one of the first Board of Directors, he devoted the energies of his great mind and heart, and the influence of his distinguished position in the Church, to the establishment and advancement of this beloved Institution. During the whole of his pastorate, and so long as he continued a member of this Board, he sought with untiring assiduity and unwavering faith, to promote, in every possible way, the prosperity of the Seminary, and the spiritual good of its numerous students,—a large portion of whom availed themselves of the benefit to be derived from his eminently spiritual and instructive ministry. The services thus rendered by Dr. Skinner during the thirteen years of his New York pastorate, must be regarded as among the most effective means of establishing the Seminary on its present strong foundations; and cannot be called to mind by the Board, without a due expression of their devout gratitude to God, for the grace that made him such an efficient helper in a time of the utmost need.

"In the year 1848, he retired from the Board and from his pastorate, to accept of the Professorship which had just been endowed, by a wealthy member of his church, with special reference to his occupancy of the chair, and to devote the undivided energies of the remainder of his life to the service of the Seminary, whose interests he had so effectually promoted. To this work he brought the ample stores of a richly cultured mind, of uncommon acuteness, in the full maturity of its powers, with large experience of pastoral life in three of our principal cities, and of a similar Professorship in Andover Seminary.

"Most faithfully and admirably did he fulfill the high expectations of the Board, in the service to which they had unanimously called him. He proved himself, not only a master in his particular department of theological instruction, but a most faithful and judicious guardian of the spiritual interests of the young men committed to his care. Most assiduously did he watch for their souls, and strive, both by his holy example and his paternal counsels, to lead his pupils into the higher walks of the divine life. Very precious is his memory to those who have enjoyed the benefits of his instructions, as well as to the Board and his brethren of the Faculty. God be praised for sparing our venerated brother, to serve Him so long in the church on earth, and for the grateful savor of his most exemplary life.

"To the family of Dr. Skinner in their great bereavement, the Board would tender their sincere and heartfelt sympathies,—congratulating them on having so long sustained to him such endearing relations, and commending them devoutly and affectionately to the all-sufficient grace of Him who careth effectually and tenderly for the widow and the fatherless."

APPENDIX.

B.

"Rev. Dr. Prentiss: "Philadelphia, June 27, 1871.

"My Dear Sir,—I have to-day your kind favor of the 26th inst., and regret that we are not to have the pleasure of that discourse from your lips, and I thank you for the kind promise of a copy of it when published. The peculiar character of Dr. Skinner will render any memorial of his life interesting, and if in the form of a biography, it would have given me pleasure to add, if possible, a tribute in token of my regard for his blessed memory.

"My first acquaintance with Dr. Skinner was at a time when he had yielded to one of the fiercest persecutions practicable in the present century. Owing to his eminent ability, his power as an orator, exalted piety and zeal, he was called immediately, on his being licensed, to be the co-pastor of the Second Presbyterian Church in Philadelphia, at that time the strongest and most influential Presbyterian church in the United States. Its pastor was distinguished as a theologian, scholar and minister. The elders of the church were men eminent in the community and of unbounded influence; the congregation large and composed chiefly of persons recognized as of the leading classes of society. The distinguishing characteristics of Dr. Skinner, which raised him to so lofty a position in the ministry, and chiefly his zeal in the work to which he had devoted himself, and his being then scarcely of age, roused a feeling in that sober, conservative congregation, most unhappy for all parties.

The young, both men and women, filled with admiration and passionate affection for the young evangelist, crowded the places of worship whenever he preached. A contrast to this, was a reality, or suspected, when the senior pastor conducted the services. A clamor arose, the like of which will probably never exist again in this country— the cry of fanaticism, wild-fire, new measures, with tales as absurd as they were false, spread over the whole city.

"The Exchange, where merchants gathered daily, the insurance offices, the banks, and every private circle rang with the name of Thomas H. Skinner, often in terms of bitter denunciation; and even now, many of the older part of our citizens, unconnected with our churches, associate his name with memories of epithets and language not to be repeated. The godly man, with all the resolution of his energetic character, sunk under the storm. Agonizing days and sleepless nights, spent in groans, were bringing him to an early grave, when his father-in-law, a wealthy merchant, with relatives of his family and a few devoted adherents, left the church and united with the Fifth Presbyterian Church, occupying a building in a very obscure position, and which under another pastor had dwindled down almost to extinction. Here, in Locust street, where the Musical Fund Hall now stands, Mr. Skinner enjoyed peace if not prosperity. He recently observed to a friend, 'From the highest round of the ladder of the pastorate, I had descended to the lowest.' It was a rest to his perturbed spirit, and here it was easy for a young man, just settling in life, to find what he deemed essential, a pew to which he could take his bride. In fact the pews, ofttimes, were more numerous than the auditors, and here Thomas H. Skinner was delivering discourses which, but a few years after, were electrifying our city.

"The building up of a church in that spot was palpably out of the question. The feeble body took its departure for a new locality; with wonderful energy and faith they succeeded in constructing a large and commodious building in Arch street, in the midst of an increasing population. From the hour when religious worship was commenced, and for years after, that church was crowded with admiring, reverential audiences. It was impossible at times for the collectors of the congregational offerings to pass through the dense crowds that filled the aisles of the church. Dr. Skinner was then in the full power of manhood, with all the fervor of youth, that lasted him indeed to his eightieth year. To others it is left to give the portraiture of this finished Christian orator. Perhaps in nothing, saving a high-wrought eloquence, in which language flowed with mingled majesty and sweetness, was he so remarkable as in his power of analysis. The most profound and mysterious problems in theology, under his preaching, assumed a distinctness and vivid clearness that astonished not less than it delighted the hearer. The conviction of truth came irresistibly, producing a deep and solemn satisfaction.

"Among the discourses of Dr. Skinner, one will illustrate his power as an orator, not more, however, than was very frequently exercised. The text was, 'Joy shall be in heaven over one sinner that repenteth.' In the scene delineated, of the sinner trespassing, and the angel group watching the fatal progress, the dramatic power displayed was perfect. With a master hand the interest was centered in the heavenly host, to whom the very thought of sin was a horror, whose holy sense of God's anger and of eternal wrath excited in them the deepest anxiety, and as the picture was drawn, the sinner advancing step by step to dreadful ruin, the mind of the audience was brought to a state of agony, when the burst of relief came, and one long sigh was breathed, and the joy was as it might have been in heaven.

"The organization of the congregation was peculiar, and very much of its character was owing to its composition. A very few members with their families constituted its nucleus. We were weak and comparatively poor. Every accession to our number was hailed with delight and received with tokens of friendship. We became associated as one family in Christ. This sentiment pervaded the whole church for years. The woman at her stall in market, and the mechanic at his bench, were greeted by the lawyer and the merchant on terms of intimacy. We sat at one table in our communion service, sitting face to face, and could not but know each other, and all this without impinging on the ordinary social differences in society. It was boldly said by a warm-hearted member, 'there never was such a church, and there never would be.' Its power in Christian enterprise was great and far beyond its supposed ability. Anything undertaken was done.

"The departure of Dr. Skinner from this scene of his labors and successes is elsewhere described, but to the last of his life he regarded it with strong regret. He walked the streets of Philadelphia with a buoyant step—for regret did not make him sad—saying, here I am at home; here was the sphere of my influence, and I never should have gone away. Others, however, think differently, and that he has exercised in the Theological Seminary an influence for good far more impressive and extensive.

"The relation in which Dr. Skinner stood towards his elder brother, forms one of the most interesting points in his life. Judge Skinner was a most honorable, high-minded man. His memoir was written by his brother—a charming production. The Judge was warm-hearted and eccentric. 'My brother Tom' was to him the Magnus Apollo; no such man, in his estimation, existed, and he loved him with the affection of a mother. A little incident was characteristic of both. Some years since, while visiting the Virginia Springs, on my arrival at the Salt Sulphur, Judge Skinner addressed me, as I dismounted from the stage coach, 'Do you know anything of my brother, and where he is?' I answered, 'He is at the White Sulphur with his family. I left him there this morning.' 'Tell me, how is it? I have been looking for him at the various springs for two weeks past, and inquiring for him in vain. On the arrival of the stage yesterday, I spoke to the most intelligent-looking man, saying, "Sir, do you know anything of the Rev. Dr. Skinner being in this valley?" He answered, "Yes; he is at the White Sulphur." "How do you know, sir?" "I heard him preach yesterday." "What," said I, "did he preach about?" After mumbling for a minute, the man said, "I don't know." I answered, "You never heard Tom Skinner preach and say you don't know what he preached about!" Tell me, now, how it is?' 'It is easily explained,' I replied. 'It was announced on the doors of the Hall, on Sunday last, that Dr. Skinner would preach. He was taken ill in the night, and I was roused at two o'clock in the morning to visit him; and having administered some soothing medicine, he was relieved, but did not leave his bed all day. Another person preached, and to-day he is well.' In his rough manner, the Judge replied, 'I knew that nobody could hear my brother Tom preach and say he didn't know what he preached about.' The brothers were together the next day, and the two remarkable men were the admiration of the crowd of visitors.

"The last I saw of my venerated friend, was on the day of Mr. Barnes's funeral, and as he parted from myself and one of his early pupils, the latter exclaimed, 'Dear old man! I love the boots he walks in!' This was but the expression of the affectionate regard in which he was held very generally by those who enjoyed his intimacy.

"I have sketched these memories of my dear friend—under whose ministry I united with the church, and from whom I enjoyed for more than fifty years the tenderest tokens of friendship—for my own gratification and at your suggestion. I do not know that they can do anything to increase, in yourself or any one, a higher estimate of Dr. Skinner than is already entertained. I suppose, indeed, they are too late for any use in your memorial of his life. Please, my dear sir, when you have done with these sheets—or rather, have read them—let me have them. I shall anxiously expect a copy of your discourse.

"Yours, most respectfully,
"JOSEPH H. DULLES."

APPENDIX.

C.

Soon after Dr. Skinner's death, a number of affectionate and grateful tributes, written by his former pupils, appeared in the religious papers. Only two of these articles are at hand; I give them both. The first comes from the shores of Lake Michigan.

THOMAS H. SKINNER, D.D.

BY REV. JAMES H. TAYLOR.

"The dear, dear old man! How I loved him! There was not the man living for whom I had such an affectionate veneration. So intellectually clear, so fiery, yet so devout, so gentle, so kind! It seems to me that if I had known he was near his end, I would have gone to New York for the privilege of passing ten minutes in his society once more. He was so simple, so sympathetic, so earnest, so interested in another's cares and joys and thinkings. His death is a personal bereavement to me. The world seems lonely in my consciousness that he is no longer in it.

"While a student under him, I learned so to love and honor him, that I have leaned upon him ever since, and have been wont to turn to him for counsel, as a son to a father. I knew, when on my way to his study, that he would not be too busy to either see me then or appoint an hour which he would give—that he would not treat my errand as a trifle, nor dismiss me with the fewest words possible, or cold expressions of opinion. Though up in the clear light himself, he would come down into a cloud or fog where another might be laboring, get round him, lay hold of him, and, if warm sympathy and clear statement would avail, he would help him out.

Possibly it may not be known to many that he was naturally *skeptical*. Surely, none who often heard him pray, and felt the wonderful power in his simple, child-like clinging to Christ, as if in a personal conference that made him oblivious to any other personal presence, would suspect anything like a skeptical cast of mind. Yet it was true. Up to twelve years ago, by the confession of his own lips to me in an interview that is still precious in my memory, such had been the life-long thorn in the flesh.

Hearing, once while I was a student, that I was in some theological perplexity, he invited me to his study, and gave me his entire evening. I had hung upon his prayers and loved him before, but never had known him until then. Such condescension, without so seeming, in turning aside from his path of light and joy, to the dark and painful way in which another was walking—such patience in wandering to and fro and pointing the way out —such tenderness and skill in disposing of difficulties! Then it was that he made known his own experience. I cannot quote exactly his language, but I can come very near it, such an impression did it make and so efficient was it for good to me. But I cannot even undertake to picture his restlessness, nervous springing, walking, and fiery words while he talked.

Said he, "I have fought the devil-suggesting-doubts every day of my Christian life. He attacks me everywhere with temptations to doubt and abandon the Christian religion. He takes every mean advantage of me. He is most likely to come when I am very weary and just dropping to sleep. Only a few nights ago," said he, "when I had lain down and was just gliding into my first doze, he whispered in my ear, 'Deny that there is any God.' And I sprang upon the floor, and cried out, 'You devil! you old coward! why take me when I am half asleep? Come when I am awake.'" Then he added, "I expect this warfare to continue as long as I live. My mind is so constituted."

But then he set forth, most impressively, the possibility of maintaining such a life of faith in Jesus that such attacks should not disturb the deep peace of the soul. He knew what such faith was. His prayers breathed it. His life was it. Blessed Jesus, who can give such victory! Nearly three-score years in the service of his Master, and loving that service more and more to the end.

He and Albert Barnes began their work together, were intimate friends, and together both have gone to their rest. Both were converted when young men studying law—both were independent in thought and bold of speech—both were charged with heresy, though only Mr. Barnes was actually brought to trial—both were too sincere and unselfish in their devotion to the Christian ministry to be soured or turned backward by opposition—both maintained unusual sweetness of spirit and singleness of purpose in their life-work. May some of us find their mantles and wear them.

Dear, dear old Dr. Skinner! We shall hear him pray no more, nor any more witness the child-like simplicity of his character in the varying circumstances of life. But we have the same Saviour who made him what he was and is.—*From the Interior, February 16th.*

The other comes across the ocean from the shores of Lake Leman.

THE LATE DR. SKINNER.

BY JAMES LEONARD CORNING.

The last post brought heavy tidings from over the sea. One after another the fathers are passing out of our sight, leaving us their examples to stimulate and reprove, and their unfinished work to be carried forward by their children. Just a score of years have elapsed since I sat in my student life at the feet of that venerable saint and scholar, whose dismission has just taken place. At that period he seemed to be an aged man, with sparse grey hair, attenuated limbs, and the deep lines of thought, mayhap, too, of sorrow, on his ample brow. Not one of all the faculty had such emphatic individuality as he. He was one of those strong characters which on the first contact impress a memory indelible by time. I remember as if it were yesterday my first introduction to him, at our matriculation in the Union Theological Seminary. In the midst of the commonplace work of taking our certificates, registering our names, and the like, some young brother proposed a theological question; and in a moment a flood-gate was lifted, and we all stood in mute astonishment at the varied wealth of learning which poured forth from his lips. There were some of our teachers whom we only dared to reverence; but I think we all loved Dr. Skinner with filial tenderness. His professional work was of such a sort which required more of the fatherly element than that of any other member of the faculty. It was his duty (a daily cross-bearing) to read over and criticise our essays and maiden sermons, to patch here and prune there with surgical pencil, to cut out adjectives and supply nouns, to shrink up our long-winded sentences and paragraphs within the limits of common sense and ordinary comprehensibility. Any school-teacher who has the weekly task of correcting a peck or so of compositions, may get just a suggestion of the amount of grace required in the function of our professor of homiletics and sacred rhetoric. For my part, I always considered him an almost solitary example of condescension and patience. A great healer of mind was he. He diagnosed our individual cases with marvelous skill. He had a remedy at hand for every intellectual infirmity. I have kept one of his prescriptions by me for twenty years. We were sitting alone in his private library, he sipping his tea and I reading sermon 'Number One,' well equipped with flights and expletives, and tied at the back with a blue ribbon. If I remember aright, he finished his tea about at the moment that I concluded the last sentence of the last "practical application." He set down his cup, and, giving me a look of paternal fidelity, said : "My young brother, your style is too florid. You must read John Foster and Isaac Taylor."

Dr. Skinner was a man of great modesty. He never paraded his learning ; and yet he was beyond question one of the most erudite theologians in the American church. He was an omnivorous reader, and it seemed that he never forgot anything. I think I know why this was so. Our class will never forget the day when he was lecturing to us on the use of books, and the almost thunder tones with which he startled us from our seats as he smote with his hand on the desk, and exclaimed : "*Young gentlemen, read with pen in hand.*" He was one of those men who back precept by example, and I have no doubt his "common-place books" of various sorts would make a good-sized library. He had one literary weakness, in that his great kindness of heart somewhat dulled the edge of his critical faculty. It has been for years a common saying among his friends that "the best book with Dr. Skinner was the last one that he read." If an author would but give him one fresh thought in a chapter, or even in a volume, the doctor was so thankful that he canonized him at once. He was altogether too merciful a man to conduct the review department of a first-class periodical.

Dr. Skinner had all the elements of a great preacher. He was a rhetorician by nature as well as by profession. And so, like all men of his class, he was in danger of sacrificing practical force to style. But he never succumbed to this subtle seduction; but was always loyal to conviction, and, as Porson has put it, 'called a spade a spade, and not a horticultural implement.' He was one of the most fervid pulpit orators that I ever listened to. It was always a marvel to me how a man, seemingly of deficient vitality, could give out magnetic force at his accustomed rate, and yet survive beyond middle-age. Nothing would explain this phenomenon but the most scrupulous physical moderation. He was temperate everywhere else but in the pulpit; but there I have often seen his earnestness rise to a pitch of "fine frenzy."

. . . .

Dr. Skinner will be remembered by all who knew him on earth as a man of extraordinary piety. Remarkable as he was in intellectual gifts, yet so great were his spiritual excellencies that the saint hid the scholar. Hence, as might be expected, his gift in prayer almost eclipsed his gift in preaching. I am afraid that, in this age of materialism and freezing philosophies, this special endowment is greatly depreciated. We have poets laureate and crowned philosophers, and it is well; but the few men and women who possess the gift of prayer in great degree are really of higher rank than poets and philosophers, deny or doubt it who will. And, above all, I love to think of our dear teacher as rarely great in the coronal element of greatness.

Every day in the lecture-room he conducted our opening devotions; and the service, though customary, never descended to formality. But occasionally a special inspiration seemed to be given him, and for a brief spell, while he voiced our sacredest thoughts and yearnings in the ear of our dear Father, we seemed caught up to the summit of some Mount of Transfiguration, and we forgot that we were still denizens of the flesh. I never will forget one fervid sentence in the midst of one of his prayers: 'O Lord, grant that every one of us may save some souls before we die!' It was a parenthesis preceded and followed by a solemn pause; and responsibility and mortality never stared us so full in the face as at that instant.

Now, as I close these honest yet imperfect words, let us for a moment think of the grandeur of moral influence. It is a sum of permutation, and no figures can compute the last result. There are probably several hundred men living to-day and occupying spheres of public influence who are chiefly or in great part indebted to Dr. Skinner for their best culture and inspiration. He was a bright jewel cast into the ocean of Time, and now sunk out of sight; but the ripples follow one another to the eternal shores.—*From the Independent of April 20th.*

VEVAY, SWITZERLAND, *March*, 1871.

APPENDIX.

D.

The following is the description referred to:

"I conclude with a brief notice of Mrs. Lowther, the mother of Mrs. Skinner. She was a grand-daughter of Governor Gabriel Johnston* and Penelope Eden, daughter of Governor Eden. Her parents were William and Penelope Dawson; her husband was Tristrim Lowther, Esq., a man of refined manners, who had a high standing at the bar, and was esteemed and beloved for his kindness to the poor and the general excellence of his character.

"Mrs. Lowther was distinguished by birth and education, in both of which she had every advantage, less than by intrinsic excellencies; such, especially, as form the highest grace and charm of the female character. Her person was a rare model of beauty and delicacy: in height, in shape, in complexion, in every feature and line so exquisitely fashioned, that, regarding it in the class of forms to which it belonged, art itself could scarcely suggest an improvement, or desire any variation; one, at least, could note no defect, could attempt no criticism, in the presence of so much that was so surpassingly beautiful and attractive. I cannot imagine that any one not insensible to beauty could see Mrs. Lowther, though in a multitude of 'the fair,' without having his eye

---

* A brother of Governor Samuel Johnston's father.

riveted by her distinctive queenly appearance, and yet she was the complete contrast of ostentatious beauty.

"The charm of all her charms was a palpably evident self-unconsciousness of being in any degree uncommon or distinctive. She could not be hid, yet it appeared to observers that she would be if she could. It gives me a singular pleasure, at this remote day, to contemplate such a specimen of unaffected modesty; I have never conceived of anything, of its kind, which I think more entitled to be termed celestial; and the adornments and movements of her person were invariably consistent with its peerless symmetry and elegance. Her dress, her steps, her attitudes, her looks, were always such as became her inherent modesty, the true dignity and nobility which belonged to her nature. For six years, during which I was an inmate of the family, according to my best remembrance of those happy years, I saw her do nothing which had not a decorum and propriety in entire keeping with her character as I have represented it. She had always a tasteful and beautiful air, and to look upon her face, or hear her voice, at any time, was a refreshment.

"And if she was so lovely and beautiful in appearance, she was more beautiful within. She did not aim at effect; if she studied to please others, as she certainly did, it was for their sake, not her own.

"It seemed to be as much her nature to be unselfish, as it is the nature of man generally to be the reverse. She always appeared—for she always was—happy in what made others so; and in the afflictions of others, how spontaneously, how sincerely, how deeply was she afflicted! When the weather was stormy, her sympathies were with the weather-beaten mariner; when the pestilence was raging, they were with sufferers, in the chamber of disease and death. I never heard her—I cannot think any one ever heard her, speak an evil word of any person. She would estimate the faults of others, and the more so sometimes, when she herself was the sufferer by them;

and if she could find no excuse for them, she would weep, and comfort herself as far as she could with that 'charity, which hopeth all things.' Her cultivation and politeness gave her no inferior place among persons of refined and elegant manners; but in intercourse with the humble and the poor, even such of them as were of lower habits, while she retained her lovely individuality, she was as familiar as if she had been one of their own class. She gave such evidence as no one could question; that she esteemed those she had intercourse with, whether of high or low rank, better than herself, and even forgot herself in the interest which she took in them. She had a bright and well-furnished mind; her proper sphere was that of the highest cultivation and intelligence; but she was quite at home, also, with persons of inferior name and condition.

"The loveliness, the grace, of Mrs. Lowther's character, as now regarded, though advanced and matured by education, was merely natural; it was what belonged to her by her original constitution as given her by her Maker. That such native excellence should have been crowned and sanctified by evangelical piety, was not a fruit from itself, and not to be on any account anticipated as a necessary or certain result. In my early acquaintance with her I do not think she was a spiritual Christian. Her goodness was constitutional, natural, not from the renewing influence of the Holy Spirit. But when the change occurred in myself, which led to a change in my choice of a profession, she was simultaneously and singularly changed; she sympathized with me in my new feelings, began a strictly religious mode of life, and, until her death, continued to give most decisive evidences of renovation by the Spirit. Her religious character was improved by time; she was a mature and established Christian when she died; and her death was serene, touching, triumphant.

"One circumstance of it was remarkably characteristic.

When the last struggle was about to commence, observing her daughter, who sat near her, overwhelmed in sorrow, she said : 'Let Maria be removed ; what is about to take place is more than she can bear.'

"She arranged her person, with her own hand pressed her falling chin upward, and so calmly and peacefully yielded up her spirit into the hands of God.

"In reviewing what I have said of a dear friend, I am not conscious of any exaggeration ; however it may appear to others, in my own vivid conviction it is but an utterance of strict sober truth. Until but a short time before her death, she lived with her daughter, the pride of the family, as she was also of the eminently cultivated and refined social circle to which she belonged."

APPENDIX.

E.

"TRULY, if ever there was a period when the whole Christian world should be down upon their faces before the throne of mercy, imploring with all the importunity and boldness and perseverance of faith, a race of ministers, each full of the Holy Ghost, as was Barnabas or Paul, that period is passing over us. Not from one place or another, but from all quarters of the earth, testimony multiplies daily that amidst the greatest possible facilities for converting the world, a greatly increased and more devoted ministry is indispensable. This testimony comes to us, not indeed as the Macedonian cry came to the apostle in a supernatural vision, but in a manner not less affecting or decisive as to its purport. It is a real sound, which flies round the land and rings in our ears all the day long. 'Send us preachers,' is the universal, ceaseless demand, at home and abroad. It comes from more than a thousand of our destitute churches; it comes from the cities, from the wilderness, from the islands, from the uttermost parts of the sea, from tracts until lately unknown to civilized man. This cry, which sounds so loudly and so complainingly in our ears, should, by general consent, be turned into prayer and sent up to heaven. And shall we longer forbear to do this? Shall we stand and hear that unusual cry, and feel no inclination to direct it to the ear of Him from whom help alone can come? Is it not a mysterious species of infatuation to forbear to lift up our cry to the Lord of the harvest? Why do we not, if this be the case, abjure the very religion of Jesus, and abandon ourselves, as well as the heathen, and the whole race of man, to despair? Why should not a reform forthwith commence, and the place of prayer have more attractions than the eloquence of any mortal, or any angel's tongue? Why, then, will not every true Christian make a covenant with himself to change his life in this particular, and from henceforth make it one of his chief subjects of wrestling supplication, that God would give us a more faithful, earnest, and laborious ministry? Why will we not call to mind how Abraham and Moses and Elias and Daniel and Paul, and, above all, how the blessed Jesus *labored in prayer*, and resolve in God's strength to pray in the same manner? Oh, what an amount of beneficent power would such prayers exert upon the external destinies of our world! What wonders of grace would be witnessed in our churches; what accessions would be made to the sacred ministry; what an impulse would be given to the cause of missions; what brightness would be shed on all the prospects of the Church!"

The following list of Dr. Skinner's publications is taken from Allibone's Dictionary of Authors:

1. Religion of the Bible. N. Y., 1839; London, 1848, '51.
2. Aids to Preaching and Hearing. Phila., 18mo; Lon., 1839, 12mo; 1840, 8vo.
3. Religious Liberty; a Discourse. N. Y., 1841, 12mo.
4. Hints to Christians. Phila., 32mo.
5. Inaugural Address. 8vo. See Spirit of the Pilgrims, vi., 84.
6. Thoughts on Evangelizing the World.
7. Religious Life of Francis Markoe. N. Y., 18mo.
8. Vinet's Pastoral Theology. Trans. and edited. 1854, 12mo.
9. Vinet's Homiletics. Trans. and edited. 1854, 8vo.
10. Discussions in Theology. 1868, cr. 8vo, pp. 287.

Dr. Skinner also published a number of religious tracts and occasional sermons, (see Fish's Pulp. Eloq. of 19th Cent., 363, 77,) and contributed to Amer. Bible Repos., Chris. Spect., Amer. Presby. and Theolog. Rev., etc.

www.ingramcontent.com/pod-product-compliance
Lightning Source LLC
Chambersburg PA
CBHW030351170426
43202CB00010B/1335